Tom Tom Corner

Travel Tales From
Around The Globe

Jonathan Moss

Introduction

IN THE HEART of Hanoi's hectic Old Quarter lies a small chaotic junction where five narrow roads converge. On one corner stands a large glass fronted store called Tom Tom, opposite, is a popular restaurant bar named Com Ga.

Above the corners bustling streets, the bar's broad balcony soon became a favourite spot, and whilst sitting there people watching the idea for this book was born.

Two months touring Europe by train gave me an early taste for travel, so six years later I set off again, this time flying Down-Under with a work visa and vague dreams of a watersports venture. Instead, I discovered the freedom and adventure of life on the road.

After a year-long meandering walkabout in Oz, I hitch-hiked much of New Zealand for six months, flew back into Australia, then took a slow route home overland through Asia. The trip lasted almost two years.

Five years on, found me backpacking through Chile, Argentina, Bolivia, Peru, and Ecuador, with an excursion to Easter Island along the way. Following six months in South America, I flew north to the States, spending the next year split between L. A., home and Hawaii.

A year later I landed a job in Grand Cayman working as a watersports instructor, but eighteen months later left the island behind and flew to Belize with hopes of starting my own business. After exploring its coast and cayes, the right opportunity never arose, so I headed to Honduras seeking work in the Bay Islands. Finally, I crossed the border into Guatemala and travelled the country by bus. After three months on the road, I returned to the UK.

Several months later I drove an overloaded van to Spain along with two friends and started a business. For the next seven years, I settled there before moving once more back to British soil.

In 2016 I spent two months travelling solo through Vietnam, crossing into Cambodia in time for Khmer New Year's crazy celebrations.

For now, I'm back in the UK…

Chapters

Introduction   iii

Australia and New Zealand   1
UFO's, Japanese Torture and Joyriding Aborigine's   3
Chasing Dollars Down-Under (P.M.A = O.P.M)   12
Five. Four. Three. Two. One. Bungy!   31
Six Months In New Zealand   38

South East Asia   61
Kelimutu: Lost and Alone on a Volcano.   63
Here be Dragons   74

China   81
Into The People's Republic of China   83
Ten Thousand Steps to Heaven:
Climbing China's Holy Mountain   92
Xian to Peking   102
Trans Mongolian Express: Six days on a train   113

South America   131
Trekking in Iceberg Territory   133
Chilean Recipe   147
Spirits of Rapa Nui   155
Flying with four wheels on the ground   165
Death Road, El Diablo and Dynamite   175

Birthplace of the Sun, Bolivian Armada and
a Brown Snouted Peruvian Pig 183
Hiking the Inca Trail 191
Bandits, Breakdowns, Condors and a Didgeridoo 199
Cactus Juice at Charlie's 209
La Selva. Coca, Ecuador 216

Hawaii 225
Aloha Maui 227

Grand Cayman 245
Swimming with Stingrays 247
Popeye Hitler and the Surf Shack 256

Central America 263
God and Jesus Alive in Guatemala 265
Chichicastenango chicken bus 270

Vietnam and Cambodia 283
A day in Danang 285
Hiding near Hue (pronounced Haway) 288
Dong Ha and the DMZ 290
Driving on the right… but usually being in the wrong! 296
Caving in Phong Nha 300
Cat Ba Island 307
The Fisherman 308
Tom Tom Corner 309
Temples, Thieves and Tuk-Tuks 313

Early Travels: Yugoslavia 321
Young. Dumb. Machine gun 323

Australia and New Zealand 1990-2

UFO's, Japanese Torture and Joyriding Aborigine's

THE TEMPERATURE WAS already over forty degrees and my slither of shade shrinking fast. Stuck at the roadside, struggling to stay in the shadow of a sign I felt I was slowly being baked alive. My thumb was getting little exercise, the day dragging and I still had two thousand kilometres to hitch.

I'd left the hostel early and a short ride took me to a helpful spot, but it had taken three long hours to get a lift to the main junction. As the gravel truck dropped me, to my dismay, I saw another hitcher already there. It was a traveller also heading for Perth, who I'd met the previous night. My plan for an early start to beat him here had backfired as he'd been lucky and got a ride leapfrogging him ahead and now he would get the next lift.

Although this was the only road leading west, I knew traffic would be light, but with little between Port Augusta and Perth, thought anyone on the road would probably be going right across the Nullarbor Plain, at least to Norsemen. Now I was at a disadvantage, and the day getting even hotter if that was possible. My tiny patch of shade soon all but disappeared.

Hitching beneath a hot sun on a lonely road is fine if you have shade. A book helps too, with the boredom. Mine, it seemed, must still be in the hostel, along with my lost sleep! With barely a vehicle going by it took a full two hours for the other guy to get a lift, by which time I'd begun contemplating hitching back to the hostel and trying again tomorrow. But even that would have been tricky with so little traffic.

At last, mid-afternoon, a dusty pale Land Rover pulled up, and the driver asked if I would share the cost of fuel. They were planning to drive non-stop to Perth, so we did a deal on the petrol, chucked my pack in the back and I climbed in.

Aussie driver Alan and his girlfriend Kelly had already picked up a passenger, a Polish guy called Adam, also going to Perth, so now all we needed to do was drive there. Just two thousand, two hundred and a bit kilometres away…

Although Australia appears sizeable on an Atlas, until you arrive on this island continent, it's hard to grasp its true scale. Three days earlier I'd travelled from Ayers Rock in the so-called Red Centre down to Port Augusta on the south coast. A fifteen-hour drive, straight down the Stuart Highway. Something just over 1250 kilometres… But despite its name the Red Centre around Ayers Rock is more like two-thirds of the way down from the far north.

The Stuart Highway is the main route running north

to south, and yet there are just seven settlements along the road, and we passed perhaps fifty vehicles in all that time. Luckily, Paul, an environmental consultant working at Yulara, Ayers Rock tourist village, had many tales to break the monotony on the long drive south.

Australia's Aboriginal people had their problems, with many alcohol, integration and social issues and were not generally too well regarded by the populace. But an Aussie mechanic discovered the local tribe had been getting one over on the white fella when he stopped to help four Aborigines seemingly stranded in a broken-down car. They asked for a tow to the next town, but the mechanic popped the bonnet to see if he could fix the problem. Immediately he saw the issue. No engine! The artful Abo's had been getting unsuspecting motorists to tow them around on outback joyrides!

WE STOPPED AT every settlement for fuel, food or cold drinks. We also made several stops to water the parched desert. Within moments of exiting the Land Cruiser, our arms, faces and legs were covered in flies.

It was astonishing; where had they come from? What did they live on out here? What had they been doing before we arrived?

We were in the middle of the vast Simpson Desert, miles from anywhere, with not another soul, vehicle or animal in sight. Why were they here? Just how many of the damn things lived Down-Under for them to find me here at this moment?

Australian flies are amongst the most persistent and irritating insects on the planet, at Yulara they would even land on your face in the swimming pool! They seem to love nothing better than exploring an inner ear, navigating up a nostril or trying to lick moisture off your eyeballs. And nothing will deter them from their quest. With a dozen attempting all three at once, it's hard not to go crazy as you stumble about doing the Aussie bush salute. A demented head-shaking, snorting, face slapping frenzy, amidst a black buzzing cloud of misery!

SETTING OFF ON the Eyre Highway was quite a daunting prospect due to the sheer distance involved, and also the fact that we would cross the notorious Nullarbor Plain. A vast, flat area where the road runs in an endless straight line through a desolate, hostile environment in which daytime temperatures regularly reach fifty degrees centigrade.

From the outset, the road was devoid of traffic and there was little to see, so to ease the monotony and help stay awake we rotated driving duties. When my turn came I adjusted the seat, accelerated through the box, and hours later realised I hadn't once touched the brakes. With that brief test done, it was up a few gears and back to the grinding monotony.

Empty blazing asphalt arrowed endlessly ahead, but our broad tyres followed every contour so I had to steer just to stay straight. It felt like driving in an old-fashioned movie set, but did help keep us awake at the wheel.

Sporadically, a sign advertising the great Aussie essentials of Ice, Gas and Beer announced a roadhouse ahead, giving the chance to stretch while Alan topped up the

⋯⋯d them for hundreds of miles, I

e would want to call one of

ɔme.

d off the road, built a fire for

fle to hunt for bush tucker,

n a few bullet-weary, sun-

arget practice. Earlier, we had

l with holes, usually pictorial

os and wombats, shot perhaps

e absence of live prey.

Alan wanted to push on, but

the risk. With something like

kangaroos hopping around

ɪg at night without roo bars is a

l kangaroos grow to six feet tall

los. Collisions can be fatal, and

ith no bars on the Land Rover,

e got a few hours rest before

tless, and again devoid of traffic.

we were g the Nullarbor Plain, an arid, desolate landscape that's indescribably dull to drive through. The road here runs in a straight line to the horizon. One stretch goes without deviation for 146 km, making it the world's longest straight. But this is dwarfed by a rail line further north which claims the record for the longest straight run of track at 478 kilometres!

Nullarbor is derived from Latin and means no trees, which is apt as there are none, for most of the way. In fact, for a thousand kilometres there is little to see on either side of the asphalt, other than sparse scrub and the odd rock. The only signs of life were a few fat carrion-eating crows, feeding on scattered chunks of baked roo bits; roadkill mowed down by mighty road trains that ply the route.

Deep-rutted tracks ploughed into the bush where tired truck drivers had dozed off at the wheel. These monstrous multi-wheeled road trains towing two or three heavy trailers stop for nothing. We gave them a wide berth whenever one approached and pulled off the road if we could. It reduced the brutal buffeting they dished out but still resulted in a less-than-brief sandblasting.

An ever-present heat haze distorted the horizon into a shimmering liquid one, and as the baked blacktop aimed unswervingly towards it, our boredom deepened. With nothing to see in any direction, kilometres clicked by slowly. But then I saw it, something odd in the distance. An incongruous low blob of colour. I squinted and blinked and thought I must be seeing things. Surely it couldn't be real. But as we drew closer, I realised it was.

A cyclist!

Out here?

He was Japanese. Of course.

Towing a trailer too. To add to his masochistic torture.

Adam nearly drifted off the road as we stared in disbelief. It was bad enough driving across, but by bike, surely it would be sheer hell. Why, why, would anyone in their right mind consider cycling. Clearly, he can't have been!

The episode kept us entertained for a while but soon the mind-numbing monotony of the road returned and we renewed our battle with boredom. We made a rare sightseeing stop at Bunda to peer over mighty eighty-metre cliffs stretching 200 km along the Great Australian Bight. Later we crossed into Western Australia and entered a different time zone, marked by the strange border town of Eucla, whose main attraction appeared to be a huge plastic whale beached on the roadside. Oddly located under a big sign advertising Emu Export lager! A second large sign read: Beware UFO's next 111 km's. We border on the unbelievable! With a population of about fifty and little else there, it was unbelievable why anyone would want to live in Eucla at all.

The Nullarbor has something of a reputation for UFO sightings and in 1988 the Knowles family claimed to have had a close encounter of the scary kind. Driving back from Perth at 2.30 am, they spotted a bright yellow light dead ahead on the empty road. As they drew closer, the light appeared to emanate from an egg-shaped object hovering just above the ground. They swerved around it, but it chased them at high speed eventually causing their tyre to blowout. Then it landed on their roof and lifted the car off the road!

Black soot and smoky gases filled the car as it got hotter and hotter inside. As the UFO hoisted them up, the terrified occupants heard their voices change, and felt their brains being sucked out. The UFO then dropped the car and disappeared, leaving the family scared and frazzled inside their blackened car. Finally, after changing the tyre, they drove to the nearest roadhouse and called the police.

The strange story attracted wide media interest, and a witness came forward who claimed to have also seen the bright light. When forensic experts examined the vehicle, black soot was found, along with dents in the roof and unexplained traces of chlorine inside the car. The police said the family had arrived in a highly traumatised state and thought "something had definitely happened out there!"

Watching footage of the Knowles TV interviews, it also appears that all four members of the family did indeed have their brains sucked out!

DAYLIGHT WAS FADING as we left the Nullarbor behind on the second day, and by the time we reached the junction at Norsemen, it was dark. The road splits here and goes north or south. Alan, however, had other ideas.

A dirt track shortcut going straight on through bush would save us about 200 kilometres and a lot of fuel, so we took it. It was a risky route, especially in the dark, but

Alan and Kelly were on holiday and hours precious, so this time Alans will prevailed.

Soon we were breathing sandy dust from the bumpy narrow track, and as we bounced around in the back, bickering started in the front. Kelly thought Alan was driving too fast, and he was clearly loving being off-road, but calmed down and slowed his pace after smashing off the door mirror on a low branch.

Luckily we encountered no roos on the track and our shortcut paid off as we joined the tarmac once more. Soon though, low fuel forced an unwanted stop in the early hours, so we parked in a servo, slept for a while and waited for the gas station to re-open.

Refuelled, but only slightly refreshed, we pushed on for Perth and arrived in the city around nine. We had covered over 2200 kilometres in forty-three hours, including the stops.

We grabbed a quick coffee, dropped Adam and drove on to a backpackers in Bulwer Street. Minutes later I was waving my friends farewell, and ready to embark on the next adventure after making the mammoth hitch across the mighty Nullarbor.

Chasing Dollars Down-Under
(P.M.A = O.P.M)

IT'S 7.30 A.M.

I'm standing amongst fifteen faces semicircled around an animated grinning manager who suddenly yells: **"How're ya'll feelin today?"**

Around me loud voices burst into chant, feet stamping and hands clapping in time.

"Fantastic. Terrific. Great. Oh yeah I feel wonderful.

Right on. Right on. Right on. Juice!

Get fired up. Juice!

Get juice fired. Fired!

Become successful and retire!

Juice to flow. Let's go.

Juice to flow. Let's go.

Juice to flow. Let's go.

Where are we going? To the top!

Where are we going? To the top!

Where are we going? To the top!

How are we going to get there?

Juice. Attitude. Motivation.

Juice. Attitude. Motivation.

Juice. Attitude. Motivation.

Whoa we all got the juice, so get fired up. Juice! Ha!
That's a fact. Jack.
Piece of cake. Jake.
Thanks for the buck. You nine-to-five schmuck.
Thanks for the money. You nine-to-five honey.
Huhh!"
!!

What the fuck is going on here? Who are these people? What are they on?

ASIDE FROM PEOPLE the room is empty, bar a few wall posters and a whiteboard. There is not a single piece of furniture. But there certainly is an atmosphere. A real buzz in the air. But it's seven thirty in the morning!

Everybody's fired up, and the room seems alive with energy and excitement. Again I wonder what everyone is on. Perhaps the 'juice' has already been flowing before I arrived!

The still grinning manager introduces the new guys, including me. Followed by "oooh he's got the shaky knees, sweaty palms, marbles in the mouth… and is gonna spit on people!!"

What IS this place? What the hell am I doing here??

FOUR DAYS EARLIER I'd replied to a small ad in the Sydney Herald. Immediate start, sales, admin, warehouse, managers. Twenty people needed. Call now…

Arriving at a nondescript office building in Alexandria I noticed that it was up for lease, which seemed slightly odd. Inside, I waited alongside a gaggle of other applicants, none of whom knew anything more than I already did. Which wasn't much. I completed a brief questionnaire and then got called in along with another candidate, which felt a little strange.

A tall green-suited Canadian greeted us, who seemed very full of himself, and absolutely full of it. In fact, he barely paused his hyped spiel to ask us any questions. A few short minutes later our interview was over, I was still none the wiser about the jobs, but had been asked back the next morning for a trial day.

Outside again, waiting with other applicants at the bus stop, the consensus was that the company must be running a scam. I for one decided I wouldn't be going back the following day. But two days and two follow-up calls later from the company, I found myself back at the office of Cobra Wholesale. Still not knowing anything about the day ahead.

As I sat stifling yawns, the sound of clapping and loud chanting came through the closed door, before it banged open and a crowd of excited people burst out. I was introduced to Hans, who would be my trainer for the day. He grabbed his holdall, and we headed for the door.

Along with dozens of others all bearing striped bags, we crowded onto a bus and headed into the city. Another short hop aboard a ferry and we arrived on Sydney's north shore where we walked into the nearest building and straight up to the first person we saw. Out of the bag appeared a flashy ten function torch. "Hi! How are you doing today? Have a look at these. They are half price. How many could you use?"!!

Throughout the day I watched in amazement as Hans relieved office girls and a few guys of their cash in return for flashing torches, lipstick sets and makeup compacts.

Hans, a blond Austrian, admittedly a handsome dude with charm and charisma, had an accent that helped and bouncing from office to office was a real blast and the bucks kept flowing in. I was amazed we were getting away with what we were doing, as we interrupted people working, sometimes even at their desks, and flogged them our stuff.

Working systematically we walked through every doorway, never missing a single one. Aside from offices, we entered any business door, be it a butchers, hardware store, police station or even a brothel! As long as it wasn't residential because they all had closed doors.

We followed a system, walking and working, covering ground and approaching plenty of people. Apparently, it was a numbers game, if you pitched to enough people a percentage would always buy. Hans seemed to be proving that.

After a long busy day, we headed back to base, which was now pumping music and buzzing with even more energy. I sat a short test about the system we followed before being called in by a manager. He seemed really enthusiastic and interested to hear about my day and after a short interview, told me I had made the grade and could start in the morning. But first I would need to buy a smart shirt and tie. Not something I'd brought for a backpacking trip around Australia where I thought I would probably be working casually, perhaps as a pool cleaner.

ALEXANDRIA WAS A bit of a mission to get to from Bondi Junction, where I was staying with friends, so I had a walk, a bus, a train and then another bus to make it by seven. Having worked in offices before I'd been accustomed to a much more civilised start time around nine! Arriving at Cobra still yawning I was met by Hans and followed him into a room full of animated people and pounding music. The space seemed alive with energy and the atmosphere felt almost electric. Everyone bar me looked wide awake and fired up, full of enthusiasm for the day ahead. Then the music died and the room quietened down as the manager Dominic walked in, and we formed a semicircle around him.

"How're y'all feelin today?"
Fantastic. Terrific. I feel wonderful.
Right on. Right on…

…

Following the chant and introductions, we went over Five Steps to a Sale.

Introduction. Presentation. Short story. Close. Rehash.

It was a simple system. (The KISS principle, keep it

short and simple) Work the territory thoroughly, see as many people as possible, get a product into their hands, qualify your buyer, sizzle the deal, close the sale, then sell them a second item. And above all, stay positive.

Positive Mental Attitude equals Other People's Money! (P.M.A. = O.P.M.)

The meeting was short and simple too, and soon everyone headed for the door. But first I had to get merched up!

Bubbly, bodacious inventory queen Ali Pye passed me a striped bag and asked what merchandise I wanted to take. I signed a responsibility docket for my stock and at days end would return unsold items and pay for what I'd sold, keeping my commission in cash. Again I headed out with Hans who gave me some final tips and left me to it, with an arrangement to meet later at lunchtime.

This was it, I was on my own… and terrified. I tested a torch for the tenth time, re-sorted the holdalls contents yet again, fiddled with my tie, walked slowly past the first door to see who was inside, before forcing myself to open it and walk in.

I approached the counter, full of nerves and trepidation, dreading marbles in the mouth and the ensuing embarrassment.

"Hi! How are you doing today? Ha-have a look at these." I stammered. "They are half price. Could you use some of those?" All the while fumbling with a crazily flashing torch which I'm supposed to get into the customer's hands!

Aside from two nights slogging around Sydney's suburbs, trying to flog shoddy art door to door with no training, I had sold nothing before. Having been dropped off in the dark and left with bundles of oil paintings, I finally managed to sell two and made a rather paltry twenty bucks in return for a lot of walking and a lot of doors closing in my face. So when I landed the job with Cobra I didn't think I would make much money but was doing it for the experience, knowing it would help me overcome my inherent shyness and build self-confidence. Also, it seemed like it might be good fun.

Unsurprisingly, I didn't sell a single thing in that first door or even in the first hour but I did make forty dollars profit that day. Which seemed amazing given the fact I felt too shy to look people in the eye whilst trying to sell them something!

The first week saw my sales steadily increase, but every day I was more impressed by the energy, enthusiasm and positivity within the office. I'd never experienced or seen anything like it. Dominic, an American, was the most motivational person I had ever met or heard. He exuded enthusiasm and positivity and was an inspirational speaker.

In daily morning meetings, following the chant, Dom got everyone fired up for the day ahead. Everything was always super positive, and it was really refreshing and eye opening to start the workday that way. Also it sounded an incredible opportunity for anyone who wanted it as a fast path led into management which was strongly encouraged. Cobra had a goal of creating ten new offices in Oz that year alone!

Each day started around seven so we could collect merchandise, practice pitching and meet with crews before someone would scream out "who wants an impact?"

This would be met with more yelling and clapping "We want an impact. We want an impact. We all want an impact. So tell us Eric baby!"

A top trainer would then run a short impact meeting, covering different aspects of the system, which would be followed by the main meeting, starting with the crazy chant! New guys would be introduced and the previous day's high rollers announced to cheers and applause.

On Monday mornings cash bonuses were handed out to whoever had met certain targets. If you made $1200 in sales, you got a shoe(wear) bonus of thirty bucks, but as a trainer with others on your crew, you could get commission overrides based on total crew sales.

I'd just arrived back at the office one Friday when a commotion erupted and I thought it was a fight. Three or four guys had wrestled another down and bound him to a swivel chair with duct tape. Moments later he got shoved out into the street to cheers and jeers before having a large smelly pie publicly pushed in his face! It turned out a bet had been made on weekly sales and this was the price of losing! The pie had been bought days before and looked rank, but this didn't stop more bets being placed for the following week!

Each night arrival back at the office was met with loud music, people charging in waving fists full of dollars and ringing the brass bell if they'd sold over $300 that day. For several weeks, I watched all of this in slightly bemused bewilderment, having come from a series of sedentary office jobs with library-like atmospheres. But then the office divided and Cobra moved to Camper-down, where, unlike Alexandria, we had no map of Sydney on the wall. So four of us walked out in different directions and started selling. For me, this was a turning point as I wandered into territory where it seemed nobody from Cobra had ventured before.

Dom had lots of sayings such as "Everyone has twenty bucks in their pocket for lunch, get it off them!" He was also a super positive person and always told us we needed to be twice as positive as anyone we met in the field. The business was all about attitude. Attitude. Attitude. Attitude.

Some days when I'd been lugging a heavy holdall, or two, around under Sydney's fierce sun it had been hard to maintain a positive attitude if sales were slow and every door was a no. But my freshly discovered territory seemed so easy I got on a roll of positivity, bouncing from sale to sale as my wallet filled. The more fun you had the more you sold, it was that simple, and the more you sold the more confident you became, so you had more fun and sold even more.

Many buildings bore signs saying No Hawkers,

which of course we all ignored, and the challenge would be to turn this negative into a positive. But our striped bags gave us away and often I would be greeted by a hostile I'm not buying anything! or Can't you read? Sometimes I would say I was conducting a survey about attitudes towards hawkers, which got a grin and broke the ice. A cheeky pommie with an accent could get away with a lot, and if you left with a smile on your face, chances are the next door would produce a sale or two. Positive mental attitude equals other people's money!

After a while, I was selling enough to burst into the office waving a wad of cash, grab the brass bell and ring it like crazy! Dom would come out to congratulate me accompanied by much back-slapping and yelling from other merchandisers and trainers. The energy inside the place was amazing. Once there, you couldn't sit down though as there were no seats. Sitting down was for the unemployed according to Dom!

As with selling, recruiting was also a numbers game, people came and went. Cobra advertised in newspapers every day, and to get as many people through the door as possible would make adverts as open and vague as the one I responded too. One even read people with long hair wanted! Or at Christmas, Santa's wanted. Always immediate start. Always multiples.

After a week many merchandisers got promoted to become trainers which meant they took out new applicants on trial days, and if that person came back and got hired, they would be on the trainer's crew.

Every evening trainers were encouraged to get with their guys to promote their situation, set goals, teach new recruits and run mini impact meetings for their crews. In this way, you could build your own organisation within the company, and once you met pre-set targets, you would be promoted to assistant manager. From there the next step would be to manager of your own office. Some people achieved this progression in a matter of months!

I soon realised that if you arrived back at the office with a new recruit, they would be hired. The test was a formality. You didn't even need a command of English. In fact, all you needed to get hired was one hand to take the cash, a shoulder to carry the merch on, and one leg to hop around the territory on!

In my first week as a trainer, I built a crew of five but all of them left the following week. This was normal. After a month only myself, Dave the shoes, Eric the frog, Robbie the fake smile remained as regulars. Slick, sharp-suited Frenchman Eric always kicked ass with his crew and the biggest weekly overrides, Dave always wore the same dodgy black and white DM shoes, and Robbie often sported a glossy magazine smile stolen from a dentist!

Thursday nights were cruise nights, time meant for team building with your crew. It was always tough to make cash though due to lack of workable (i.e. open) territory. But it could be a laugh, especially when we had screeching monkey sleeve puppets for sale. Stick your hand up their bum and they howl seemed to be one of

Dave's favourite selling pitches! And five young Brits bursting into a Sheila's hair salon wearing hand puppets singing "Hey hey, we're the monkeys" was great for morale even if we didn't sell any. Or get any phone numbers!

Friday nights were International Beer Nights. On the company. In all of its many offices around the world. So a cold slab or two of VB amber nectar would be waiting in the Camperdown office, contrasting with the rest of the week when you were lucky to get a cup of water from the cooler! A few of us always snuck back early to hide a few tinnies to ensure a steady supply before heading off to the nearest bar.

The downside of International Beer Night was that Saturday was also intended to be a team-building cruise day. Which never seemed to go well when you'd woken hungover, slumped in a car at the roadside somewhere, along with three Cobra crew having failed to find the route home. All of whom had to be back at work in another hour!

Working for Cobra felt a little like joining a cult in so much as the time commitment we were encouraged to make. Every day was a minimum of ten hours and often more, plus the travelling. Phil and Jo, my flatmates, started to worry about me as they hardly ever saw me, or perhaps they were just being polite!

On Sundays I would shop for food, iron my shirts and fall asleep, shattered. But I was hooked on the opportunity. People within the organisation were making serious money. Cobra was just a small part of an international company operating in dozens of countries and close to a hundred cities. Sydney hosted a multinational rally, and I watched a manager get presented with a cheque for over $100,000. His bonus for that year. One of the vice presidents picked up his annual bonus too. One point one million dollars!!

In Camperdown, the only things on Cobra's walls were people's goal sheets. These displays of what merchandisers wanted generally had glossy magazine pictures of models of three types: fast cars, fancy boats and bikini-clad females! Before Cobra, I thought a goal sheet was something football related.

Listening to stories at the rally I realised what was possible. Dom was a year younger than me, but at 26 had the goal to retire by 30! The company presidents sounded like they were making fortunes. It all seemed attainable. Supercars. Super-yachts. Supermodels. And more.

OUR MERCHANDISE CHANGED by the week or depending on how fast we could sell it. It never failed to amaze me how many torches we sold to the citizens of Sydney, or calculators or lipstick sets (ten for ten dollars!) Plastic portfolios, kitchen knives, belts, microwave pots, makeup compacts, musical dolls, solar radios, foil pictures and monkey puppets. And everything half price!

Well, maybe it wasn't, but I didn't learn that for some time. The owner imported the merch and sold it to

Dom, who sold it to us. We then sold it to anyone with some cash! It wasn't much different to shops using m.r.r.p's, which of course isn't the retail price.

The trick was to stick with the system, work your territory thoroughly, never prejudge a sale, be super positive, get a product into their hands, qualify the buyer and not waste time trying to persuade people. If the person you were pitching to didn't even look at the product, let alone take it, you knew right away they weren't interested. No worries mate, have a good one, see ya…

With some merch though it was so easy to get them to take it. Hi, how are you doing? Have a look at these. Catch! They are half price…

Many offices in the city didn't seem keen on having us loose in the building selling and distracting their worker ants, so the challenge became to beat the security by having two people working alternate floors and hopping up or down a few levels in the lift if security spotted you. Unlike us, for some reason, guards never seemed to see the funny side. These buildings were full of people with lunch money, so the potential was huge, if somewhat challenging!

I liked working hospitals because of their high numbers of staff and also having worked in a hospital back home I knew which departments to hit. I had so much success in them I became known as Doctor Moss at Cobra until hospital security caught and unceremoniously evicted me with threats of court action for further incursions!

Despite making good money as a regular top merchandiser, I couldn't keep a crew for long and the opportunity for the next step towards management remained distant. Also, I had come to Oz to explore and travel, not to just work, so decided to quit the company and hit the road instead.

I gave notice that I would leave in a month which resulted in my deck getting loaded. In an effort to keep me I got given two or three trainees a day in the hope I would build a crew. But selling became almost impossible with four people crowding around a counter facing the person cowering behind it.

I was set on leaving and needed all the money I could get for months of travel, so my solution was to explain straight away what we would be doing, knowing full well ninety percent of people hired lasted less than a week anyway. Those interested stayed with me, but many left. Some even before we reached the bus stop!

BEFORE LEAVING I led a road trip to Newcastle along with three others temporarily on my crew. Arriving early I noticed a rusty battered relic of an estate car parked outside and said I hope that's not the hire car. But alas, it was. The name of the company said it all really: Rent a bomb!

We crammed 800 musical dolls inside filling all but the front seats to capacity. Little space was left for our own luggage, let alone for more crew members, so two had to travel up by train. Despite the dolls being tightly packed every time we hit a bump they played irritating tinny tunes, driving us crazy all the way up the coast.

Leaving the office we'd needed fuel, so I pulled into the nearest garage and climbed out, loudly complaining about the piece of crap hire car. At which point the attendant said returning or extending? Sorry? I replied. Returning or extending? What? Are you returning or extending your rental he said… Shit, sorry mate I didn't realise it's your car! Fortunately he wasn't angry or insulted, as after all I'd only told the truth, and later said don't worry if it gets more dents, they all add character!

Joining us was a crew from the books division, whose dilapidated van had so much weight in the back that turning the wheel had little effect and was down to first gear on many hill climbs, resulting in a long slow crawl north. Remembering the rental guy's words I made the boring drive more entertaining at traffic lights by sometimes ramming the back of the van!

Approaching town a rear van tyre blew out under the load, and the jack was buried under dozens of boxes of books. An Aussie stopped to help but soon regretted his decision when the weight destroyed his jack. The AAA arrived and told the book boys their van was dangerously overloaded and shouldn't be driving anywhere, but as we were really close to our destination, he reluctantly helped them back on the road. At last, we pulled into Newcastle, unloaded everything into storage and checked into a caravan park.

THE TRIP TURNED out to be a huge success, helped by the fact it was the run-up to Christmas. The dolls almost sold themselves. All I had to do was stroll in winding up a few, line them on the counter and smile as they waggled their heads and played tunes. Girls loved them. Oooh, they are soo cute, I want one, how much are they? I didn't need to pitch half of the time and just stood back making silent sheep noises as I watched the herd mentality take effect. Ooh, are you having one? I think I will get one too. Me too. I want one as well. And me...

If I could get past the receptionist, who'd often say she thought no one would be interested, all it would take was just one person to want one, then the other sheep would follow. The receptionist would bring back the doll with the order and then decide she wanted one too. Baaa!

By the end of the week we had sold every working doll and set a record for a road trip, so went out to celebrate. The problem was I had so much cash stuffed into my pockets it was tricky to pull out single notes as I hadn't had time to bank the final day's takings, and certainly couldn't leave them in the caravan!

THE VAST MAJORITY of Cobras recruits were young travellers, mostly under 25, and a real mixture of nationalities. At various times I had people from Fiji, Tonga, New Zealand, Spain, Taiwan and Vietnam on my crew. One couple, an American called Helmut, and his Scottish girlfriend Viv told me about a traveller who'd hired a kangaroo costume and made good money busking outside the Opera House. So we decided for a laugh to give it a go and maybe make some cash too. We couldn't find a roo suit, so hired a huge furry koala outfit complete with four-foot tail and headed down to the harbour.

The Opera House is Sydney's most iconic landmark and sits at the end of Circular Quay facing the imposing Harbour Bridge, a.k.a the Coat-hanger. So it seemed an obvious place to busk, and yet nobody was busking when we arrived. Despite the kangaroo story, I couldn't believe we would get away with what we had planned. But what the heck, we had paid for the suit…

Ten dollars for a photo didn't go down too well with the tourists, so our cheeky charge soon dropped to a dollar donation for the costume. With Helmut or myself zipped inside the koala, the more we bounded about the quicker the bucks rolled in. Chasing and pouncing on people, play fighting with kids or simply messing about putting on a show. We then posed with the tourists and Viv took a picture on their camera. Come and have your photo taken with the mad koala man!

Japanese tourists in particular couldn't get enough of it, but we soon gave up trying to steer them so the Coat-hanger or Three Nuns in a Scrum was in the background of their photo.

It was sweltering inside the suit, so we swapped every half hour to rest the koala man, but it was so much fun and we took $200 in just a few hours. The police saw and ignored us, but probably didn't realise what we were up to. We had such a laugh that Viv and Helmut quit Cobra to become the mad koala man full time. They lasted a week before the police realised they were busking and moved them swiftly along!

THERE WAS ANOTHER street performer who I sometimes spotted. Dressed as a garden gnome he sat motionless holding a cane with a line going down into a drain. Intrigued, I watched for a while but he only continued to fish. He looked to be making lots of money, so I thought he must be good whatever he was doing. Despite watching several times I never saw him move and yet his hat was always full of cash. Months later in a different city, I met another busker and mentioned the gnome. It turned out they knew each other, so I asked what the gnome did to make so much money. Oh, nothing he replied, he just fishes. But now when he gets bored with the watching crowd he lifts the rod and out of the drain pops a little card saying Piss Off!

P.M.A. = O.P.M.
It even works for an urban fishing gnome!

Five. Four. Three. Two. One. Bungy!

ICE CRYSTALS GLISTENED on the gangplank. Poking into thin air the narrow wooden stub jutted at right angles from an ageing suspension bridge spanning a sheer-sided gorge. Two hundred and twenty-nine feet below a few inches of clear, frigid water barely covered the gravel riverbed. With ankles bound I let go of the rail and shuffled forward, but felt a stab of fear as my soles had little grip. The last thing I wanted was to slip off and fall. I wanted to dive off and fall!

SIX MONTHS EARLIER aboard an air-conditioned bus heading for Brisbane, I spotted a towering bungy crane on a beach near Surfers Paradise. Its draw was irresistible. I backtracked down the Queensland coast and soon found myself sitting on Death Row alongside some fellow adrenaline junkies, waiting for ankle straps to be tied on.

"Nice and tight please!" said the bloke in front. The bungy guy just laughed at that. "Not too tight thanks mate." I said. He grinned and loosely wrapped the straps around my ankles.

"No worries mate, she'll be right. Gravity will take care of that!"

There was no escaping now, not that I wanted to. I'd watched a handful of jumps and the big rubber band looked fairy strong. What could go wrong!

I hopped across into the cage, got clipped to the bungy cord, the gate closed behind me and the crane hoisted us heavenwards. Sandy beach spread wide as the cage climbed higher. And higher. A hundred and fifty feet below, my friends appeared the size of ants. From the top of the crane, my view was incredible, but the drop daunting. "Don't look down mate." Too late!

"Remember to look to the horizon when you dive." The cage door opened. I shuffled forward and waved the world goodbye. With toes curled over the edge, the countdown began.

"Five. Four. Three. Two. One. Bungy!"

I dived out and plummeted at the ocean. Seconds later I shut my eyes as I hit the surface before being yanked skywards. Feet first, accelerating up a hundred feet or more, floating mid-air for a millisecond, then falling. The second rebound rocketed me back at the crane, spinning and twisting at the whim of the elastic before plunging towards the sea. Adrenaline overloaded my system, making it almost too intense to take everything in. Crane, sky, beach, water. Crane, sky, water, crane. The recoiling bungy cord see-sawed me up and down until I felt myself being slowly lowered to the crash mat. Grinning from ear to ear and buzzing from the rush all I wanted was to go straight back up and jump again!

Instead, I got handed a glass of champagne and a certificate which read: Jon Moss being of sound mind did of his own choice plunge from a 150ft platform headfirst to the Broadwater, Gold Coast Australia, bound only by a wing and a prayer and a bungy cord and is duly awarded the Diploma in super sports achievement!

At that moment I decided I had to go to New Zealand. Home to the world's biggest legal bungy jump.

BUNGY JUMPING IS thought to have been started centuries ago by natives of Vanuatu in the South Pacific. Leaping from bamboo towers attached only by vines tied around ankles was the ultimate test of bravery and believed to ward off evil spirits and ensure a successful yam harvest!

Three years ago in 1988 AJ Hackett started bungy jumping commercially in New Zealand, following several pioneering jumps made by members of the Oxford University Dangerous Sports Club. They made their first from Clifton Suspension Bridge, but after the jump, all got arrested! More jumps followed in the States including one from the Golden Gate Bridge, raising awareness and interest in the new adrenaline sport. A.J Hackett then grabbed more headlines with a high profile jump in Paris from the Eiffel Tower, whereafter he was also taken into custody!

BY THE TIME I reached Queenstown, the bungy capital,

in New Zealand's breathtaking South Island, winter had arrived, and it was bitterly cold. But once I'd found accommodation I headed straight to A.J's shop. Despite freezing temperatures, trips out to the Canyon were running, and I soon had an Air Ticket clutched in hand.

Jump day dawned and by seven thirty I was waiting outside Hackett's downtown hq. It was cold, dark and lashing down but I felt wide awake and hyped up. After being weighed and signing a waiver, I clambered aboard a plush Land Rover and set out for Skippers Canyon. As the road climbed higher out of Queenstown snow replaced rain, but we pushed on. Soon we left tarmac behind, engaged four-wheel drive and joined the treacherous canyon road. A road deemed so dangerous that no rental cars are covered here.

The old mining track had been blasted from the mountainside, and on one side sheer drops plunged to the Shotover River below. Several times our driver pulled over near particularly high precipices and taunted us saying "that drop is small compared to the jump site!" A helpful chap.

Following the tortuous icy track snaking through spectacular alpine scenery, the snow flurries eased and, at last, the skies began to clear. We reached Skippers Canyon bridge and walked across. The drop over the side was intimidating, tingeing my excitement with the first touch of fear. Far below the river looked just inches deep. There was no margin for error.

Miles from habitation and surrounded by snow-capped peaks, the 90-metre long historic wooden bridge spanning the ravine was in a dramatic setting but that did little to distract from the thought of what I was about to do.

Once everything was ready, one of AJ's crew clipped in and took a dive. The drop was phenomenal, his free-fall endless, the rebound mind-blowing. Three other jumpers followed. And then it was my turn.

I sat whilst ankle wraps were applied and couldn't keep my eyes off the drop. I started to shake with excitement, probably mixed with some fear too. A jet boat arrived below, so now I had an audience. The jumpmaster told me to calm down and gave final instructions:

"Don't look down. Look towards the trees opposite. Let's have a nice dive, straight at the trees. Get your toes right over the edge. Now wave for the camera."

Then the countdown began.

"Five. Four. Three. Two. One. Bungeeeeeeey!!!!"

I threw my arms forward and pushed hard from my feet diving out and away from the platform. Instantly I hurtled head first at the gravel. Rock faces blurred as I plummeted past. In seconds I was free-falling at 160 kph. The shallow river rushed up at me. Much too fast. Then, deceleration. A micro pause... and catapulted skywards. Yanked feet first, accelerating back at the bridge. A massive, intense rush, mainlining adrenaline.

After the first rebound, I took more in. The free-fall, the speed, the river, the snow covered rocky gorge, the helpless rag doll rebounds and the wild spinning, flung about at the mercy of elastic. Every cell in my body was buzzing with the intensity of the experience.

The recoils decreased until I was left swinging, hanging head-first before being lowered into a waiting jet boat. Moments later my feet were back on the ground standing on a shingle bar craning up at the bridge. Full of adrenaline I leapt about laughing like a lunatic with a crazy grin spread across my chops. The height of the bridge looked insane from below and I had just jumped off it!

As I watched two jumpers tried the Elevator, a backwards pin drop plunging feet first before being whipped around and catapulted back up. The speed of their drops was instantaneous, almost straight into terminal velocity.

I wanted to jump again but didn't have the funds, so clambered aboard a jet boat and tore through the narrow canyon to rendezvous with our Land Rover.

All jumps had been videoed, so I was itching to get into town to watch mine.

Halfway back we came across a Land Rover that had slid over the edge, luckily for the driver a tree had prevented a lethal plunge, but there was little we could do other than offer a lift. His trip along the canyon road had turned out to be even more expensive and scary than ours!

Back in town I watched my jump over and over and collected a certificate for joining the Canyon Club. It read that I 'had lost all touch of reality and sense of responsibility towards life in throwing themselves off a bridge 229 feet above a rampant, raging river attached to nothing more than a great big rubber band!'

ONE WEEK LATER I was standing in line waiting to throw myself off another Queenstown bridge…

As the marketing says: AJ Hackett Bungy – Jump with the professionals, you'd be crazy not to!

Six Months In New Zealand

North Island

AUCKLAND'S INLAND REVENUE Office seemed an unlikely place to start an adventure, but I'd heard of a possible loophole in their system. My six-month tourist visa did not allow me to work but if I could obtain a tax file number and find a job, I could claim to be a kiwi and pay income tax like a good citizen!

Approaching the counter I held my nerve, handed over the forms and shortly afterwards made a hasty exit along with a newly issued tax file number! With the paperwork completed I didn't waste much time before heading north, but was only kilometres from the city when a police car pulled up, and it seemed unlikely they wanted to offer a lift, despite my optimistic thumb thrust in the air.

What the hell did I think I was doing? the officer demanded. Errr… hitchhiking.

Apparently, hitching was illegal where I stood and the fine 500 dollars. Fortunately, they let me off as my first ride had crossed the Harbour Bridge then left me on the motorway, so I had no option but to keep hitching. Relieved it was unrelated to the dubious acquisition of a tax file number I didn't protest when they failed to offer a lift, despite leaving me a long backpack-laden slog to a legal spot!

After the false start, hitching seemed easy, and I wound my way steadily north with a succession of lifts taking me to Whangarei, Russell, Paihia and on to Kerikeri in the beautiful Bay of Islands. The further into Northland I hitched the more dramatic the scenery became, and we drove dirt tracks through lush green landscapes devoid of either habitation or people.

In Kerikeri, I booked into Aranga Park and put my name on the kiwi-fruit pickers waiting list. Days later my cheeky visit to the IRS paid off when the suspicious chargehand asked if I had a work visa. Here's my tax file number I replied and handed him the paperwork!

With that, I landed six weeks picking work and joined an international gang stripping little green hairy fekkers from local orchards and giving a slice of my pocket-money straight to the government.

When the short season finished, I drove an ancient Toyota to Auckland for one of the pickers. With no requirement for an MOT, his neglected vehicle was a death trap, with dangerously vague steering and barely any brakes. Surprisingly, the battered hatchback made it back to the city where I spent a few days before hitching south.

I'D MET NICOLA in Mt Eden backpackers and we were standing roadside with thumbs stuck out when a car veered towards us. As it skidded past, I pulled her from its path before the driver slid to a stop and offered a lift! We had our doubts, but it was raining hard so squeezed inside. It was then I noticed the driver was missing a hand!

Apparently he'd lost it in a recent farming accident and had a primitive metal hook in its place. He could barely use the hook, but it didn't slow him in the slightest as we sped erratically over soaked tarmac. Every time he changed gear, he let go of the wheel with his right hand and reached across to grab the gear stick! It was a hairy ride, and we felt very relieved he didn't drive us far.

Unlike Northland, hitching was hard, and we struggled to get lifts. By the time we stepped from the seventh car it was dark and it had dropped us at a deserted junction. The next town was too far to walk, so we could do little but stay put and hope something showed up. After a long cold wait, a driver on a late post run pulled up and drove us to Putaruru.

The small town had few rooms to offer, so we ended up staying in what seemed to be a halfway house, full of very strange folk. One inmate immediately latched onto us giving fashion shows modelling all his clothes! Double door bolts ensured the night passed without further incident and next morning we paid up and promptly escaped the asylum.

Two lifts later we rolled at last into Rotorua and were greeted with the strange sight of rising steam and a noxious smell of sulphur pervading the air. Danger

Steam! warned road signs. Plumes could be seen all around, even belching from drains, giving the unusual town a slightly sinister feel.

The region sits on a volcanic belt and signs of geo-thermal activity were everywhere. Lake Rotorua felt warm to the touch, our hostel boasted a thermal tub and opposite the hospital, boiling mud pools had just been fenced off to prevent more terminally ill patients from taking a gruesome final bath.

ROTORUA IS HOME to the scenic Skyline gondola that runs to the summit of Mt Ngongotaha. A ride in a Skyline cabin also takes you to the top of the Luge, a steep, crazy, concrete Cresta-run snaking down moun-tainside for a kilometre.

The fast winding course has wide banked turns which can be attacked almost flat out. Sitting atop a low-slung wheeled sled with handlebars I careered down the slope carving berms and chicanes and taking off over jumps. There seemed little concession to safety, and the speed meant any mistake could be punished with being spat from the track and launched into rocky scrubland!

It was a test of nerves to see how late you could brake to still make the bend. Nicola didn't seem keen on the speed or lack of safety, so after a few runs we called it a day and left the mad mountain track behind.

Next morning we set out with Doug and his dog, Mickey the Rat, from Tarawera Tramping Trips and four fellow backpackers to explore Waiotapu Thermal

Wonderland. A smouldering other-worldly park of boiling mud pools, craters, geysers and simmering lakes of steaming water.

Strange gurgling sounds and bubbling noises slipped from the eerie steam-enshrouded primaeval landscape. Large areas looked like visions of hell, and had names such as Devils Bath, Devils Ink-Pots and the Devils Home. Lady Knox Geyser sprayed warm water 20 metres in the air when she furiously erupted, creating myriad ever-changing rainbows. Close-by, Inferno Crater spat scalding globs of mud skywards, and in the ochre-ringed Champagne Pool boiling water bubbled without pause from bottomless depths.

Climbing back into the old Land Rover we crawled up steep winding tracks to the top of Mt Tarawera for a long crater walk. In the late 1800s this immense volcano erupted burying several Maori villages and killing more than a hundred people. Three peaks erupted together resulting in a massive 17 km fissure being ripped from the summit, leaving behind spectacular plummeting slopes of red scoria.

Despite dire warnings from Dougie, temptation proved too strong, and we scree-jumped hundreds of feet down steep loose slopes into the bowels of the dormant volcano. Just the previous week a backpacker doing the same had broken a leg and proved tricky to extricate and Doug did not want a repeat performance. The wild run felt worth the risk, but made the long climb out a lot tougher on tired shaky legs!

FROM ROTORUA WE continued hitching south, stopping overnight at Hastings in Hawke's Bay. A friendly kiwi who'd picked us up at the roadside offered a room for the night, but his wife wasn't so welcoming when we arrived unannounced, and a row kicked off in the kitchen.

A large pizza pacified her briefly, but next morning we left early along with her husband who seemed equally eager to escape! He took us to the top of Te Mata Peak, where below our vantage point, lush green hills rolled south and a wide sparkling expanse of the bay stretched north.

Six hours and three lifts later we reached Wellington and checked into an exposed wooden hostel set on the side of a hill. New Zealand's capital is known as the windy city and was living up to the name when we arrived. During the small hours of our second night, I got woken by the room shaking and thought wow this really is windy here before dozing off again. Next morning when we checked out I learned the shaking wasn't caused by wind, but by a sizeable earthquake centred just outside the city!

South Island

ARATIKA, THE INTERISLANDER ferry, took us across Cook Strait, through the glorious Marlborough Sounds and on to the terminal at Picton on the South Island. The three-hour crossing had a reputation for rough weather, but we were blessed with clear blue skies and calm waters.

We wanted to travel down the sparsely populated west coast, but as hitchhiking was rumoured to be hard, booked seats on the Westcoast Express running to Queenstown. So started a six-day adventure aboard a tired old Leyland bus bursting with backpackers, booze and loud music.

Lush valleys, wild rivers and mountain passes make the west coast scenically spectacular, with one road section carved from a sheer rock face where our bus barely scraped through. The unspoilt coastline hugging the Tasman Sea is home to seal colonies, pancake-like stacks of rock and explosive blowholes showering salty spray high overhead.

Stopping in the township of Blackball, we checked into the Hilton, an old wooden building straight out of the wild west and a relic from gold rush days. After the gold came coal, and a mine opened, but in 1908 an illegal three-month strike led to miners being sent to court. Ironically, or perhaps arrogantly, the presiding judge adjourned for lunch for forty minutes, when the miners were striking about extending their own lunch breaks from fifteen minutes to thirty!

FURTHER SOUTH WE found glaciers and hiked to the Franz Josef following the course of milky glacial flour flowing from its face. Constant glacial movement grinds rocks beneath it so finely that rock flour is held in suspension in meltwater, resulting in its milky appearance.

Early next morning we visited Lake Matheson whose silky-smooth waters provided a giant mirror to perfectly reflect majestic snow-capped peaks overlooking the picturesque lake. Later, we hiked through dripping fairytale rainforest, where giant tree ferns and hanging mosses gave a feel of land that time forgot. Crossing a precarious, rippling swing bridge one person at a time, we prayed nothing would break on the ageing wood and wire structure, strung fifty feet above an icy raging torrent.

After lunch, I joined a group heading to Fox glacier, but first, we had to try to bump start an ancient tour bus meant to be taking us there! After a change of coaches, we finally made it to Fox carpark and set out on foot.

Wielding alpine walking staffs and wearing metal-studded boots and we hiked up on top of the glacier. Chopping steps with his ice axe, our kiwi guide led us past plunging blue crevasses, ice caves, drip holes and wavelike formations caused by the glaciers constant movement.

Squeezed between jutting snow-capped peaks the spectacular ice river rose steeply above us, and below, its gouged course snaked through boulder-strewn valley floor. Beneath our frozen boots lay ice three hundred feet thick.

Both Fox and Franz Josef are fast-moving glaciers and an aircraft that crashed in 1943 onto Franz Josef took just over six years to reappear at its terminal face. A movement of one and a half metres a day. More recently the glacier advanced a full five metres in a single day!

Next day a deserted coastal road wound past yet more waterfalls, through lush, dense rainforest and on to the crystal clear Blue Pools, home to plump, cruising brown trout. Later, our old bus struggled to climb the spectacular Haast Pass where tarmac clings to the mountainside with sheer drops plunging hundreds of feet to a rock-strewn river gorge below.

Ending the day at Makarora mountain camp I hiked a flood-ravaged river course, rock hopping upstream through a boulder and tree trunk strewn gully until an unscalable rock wall brought my adventure to a halt. Back at base camp, a large barbie had been laid out, along with more beer to celebrate our last night, so before long the drinking games began!

Our final day dawned and the Westcoast Express took us to Wanaka, nestled beside a beautiful lake sharing the name, before driving on to Queenstown. But just before arriving in the bungy capital our driver stopped at Kawarau Gorge to allow several passengers to throw themselves off a bridge attached to large elastic bands!

OVERLOOKED BY THE Remarkables mountain range, Queenstown's location on the shores of Lake Wakatipu is spectacular, with the aptly named snow-dusted peaks colours changing throughout the day. Aside from the powerful draw of the bungy bridges, I was hoping to find work in local ski fields, but the snows were late and the town full of travellers with the same idea as me. After a week of bungy jumping, jet boating and waiting, the snow still hadn't arrived, so I hitched south to Te Anau, then took a bus to Milford Sound.

From Te Anau the road runs through a glacial valley surrounded by more snow-dusted peaks, passing mirror lakes and frigid, boulder-strewn rivers. But ice made road conditions lethal and when our coach almost slid off the side, the driver resorted to snow chains.

As he fitted the chains an inquisitive Kea showed up in hope of a free snack. These cocky alpine parrots can be real pests due to their destructive habit of pecking bits off vehicles and stealing anything that takes their fancy. Fortunately, this one seemed content with a few crisps tossed down by a Japanese tourist.

Emerging from the dynamited Homer Tunnel darkness the road descended past towering rock faces stained black by near-constant waterfalls. After 120 kilometres of breathtaking scenery, we arrived and rendezvoused with waiting Red Boats. Stretching before us was a sublime vista, with snowy peaks plunging vertically into the inky placid waters of Milford Sound. In the middle, rising to 1700 metres, jutted majestic Mitre Peak.

Our skipper took a meandering course along the spectacular 22 km fiord out to the mouth of the Tasman Sea, stopping en route to fill champagne glasses beneath an icy waterfall showering from hundreds of feet above. Later, as we cruised towards dock, dolphins played on our bow-wave as curious seals languidly swam by. Ashore, as the bus drove back to Te Anau, a fiery orange sunset behind silhouetted peaks providing a fitting ending to the trip.

MORE LIFTS LED me west to Dunedin where I stayed in a garishly painted hostel that shouldn't have made it past planning! Its interior was just as lurid with yellows, greens and turquoise generously splashed around. A red English phone box resided in one corner with a rustic shack supported by dead trees in another. Battered, rusting tin cans and hanging boots decorated its branches and old bicycles dangled dangerously from ceilings! Travellers graffiti from around the globe covered the walls, a commode sprouted a palm and in pride of place sat an old barbers highchair!

Close to Dunedin is the Otago Peninsula which homes an albatross colony at Taiaroa Head, so along with two fellow travellers, I decided to cycle out to see them. Our vague plan turned out to have a flaw as we hadn't taken into consideration the consumption of so much Steinlager the night before. Leaving the hostel considerably later than planned, an easy level road led along unspoilt coastline around bays and headlands towards Taiaroa. En route an isolated pub delayed us further as cycling had made us thirsty again and they served a fine Steinlager!

Finally, after three hours we reached the colony and were rewarded with the sight of a downy royal albatross chick. Perched on an exposed cliff top the pure white fluffy youngster looked the size of a small sheep. Already weighing in at several kilos, it was patiently awaiting more food, but neither parent returned as the wind was too light for them to land. With a wingspan of over three metres royal albatross, or toroa, are the largest seabirds in the world and renowned ocean wanderers, travelling up to 190,000 km in a single year!

We'd been told a beach 10 minutes away was home to rare penguins, so pushed on for that. But ten minutes turned into thirty so by the time we arrived, it was too dark to see much more than a few indistinct shapes waddling across sand. Soon it was pitch black, and as we started back up the steep bumpy track, Wills chain broke with a loud crack. We had no lights, were 30 odd kilometres from Dunedin, and now had one bike down!

We coasted, paddled or pushed until finally head-lamps appeared. The driver thought the pub may have a phone so offered to run Will back there. But despite having space inside his campervan, left Ant and I to ride 11 km down the dark and now icy dirt track! We eventually found Will still in the pub, so joined him for yet more Steinlager until the bike's owner, Scott, showed up and drove us back to the hostel.

Scott was running a conservation project on part of his land and offered a visit in return for some work. So next day we headed to the yellow-eyed penguin colony and helped with habitat conservation work. As dusk fell, we crept closer to the beach and watched a dozen penguins emerge from the water. The rare birds looked rather incongruous waddling up a sandy beach and on through grassy dunes.

Laying sprawled on the sand was a large, equally rare, bull hooker sea lion and we belly-crawled to within metres, ready to run if it looked likely to charge. But as we were downwind and in low light, he didn't notice us. Both species are only found in New Zealand and numbers sadly in decline. With less than 500 left, it felt a privilege to share the sand with them.

Scott, like most of the kiwi's I'd met, was friendly and open and kindly invited us back home to share 'fush and chups' with his wife and family.

OVER THE NEXT few days, I hitched north getting lifts from more helpful, friendly locals. Kiwis generally seemed so proud of their country and were always keen to show it off, one driver even detoured for sightseeing and ice creams, but his musical taste marred the long ride. He played one tape containing his one favourite song non-stop for the duration!

More lifts led me to Christchurch, where I booked into Pavlova backpackers, but with no ASB bank in town I couldn't access any cash and was down to my last few dollars. I spent a fruitless week looking for work, awaiting a money transfer from the UK. The large hostel was a transient place, meaning plenty of free food got left in the fridges, and I vacuumed acres of carpet in exchange for my bunk.

Nearby Cathedral square provided daily entertainment from a host of pious speakers ranting fervently atop little soap boxes, bibles clutched in palms. The central square also homed chanting orange-robed Hare Krishna devotees, an array of street performers and predatory Scientologists who were best given a wide berth! When at last my funds arrived, I left the city behind and headed out to a farm stay along with new friends Dave and Jo.

HITCHING NOW BECAME much harder with three people and packs to fit inside, so it took a long time to reach the Banks Peninsula. Finally, on the last leg our new host, Peter drove by and picked us up but then stopped soon afterwards at a lonely mist-shrouded beach. Huge mounds of pebbles blocked the route, so we shouldered packs and hiked into the mist, eventually finding another vehicle parked on the far side which Pete drove to the farm!

Our outdoor accommodation was freezing, with holes in the floor and gaps in the walls, so the first job was to repair the old shearers shed. The drafty wooden shack had no power, light or heat but we threw down an old carpet and nailed boards over cracks in the walls. Despite our best efforts, we still ended up sleeping fully clothed every night.

Our host family made us feel welcome at the remote hill station, and at first, we split logs and did odd jobs in return for food and board. There wasn't really enough work but shearing season was nearing a start, so we hitched to Akaroa for several days, before returning to Hoggets Farm to work in the sheds.

Working with sheep seemed like fun as we drove them, yelling and clapping, between pens, but soon their stubborn nature made it frustrating when they refused to budge or all bolted at the last second. And with the threat of shaved heads hanging over us, the pressure was on to provide the fast-working shearers with a constant supply!

When shearing finished, I left Dave and Jo and hitched back to Christchurch to go snowboarding, getting picked up early morning then heading for the ski fields at Porter Heights.

It was my first time on a snowboard and several wild, cartwheeling wipeouts soon calmed my need for speed, but my main problem was the drag lifts. With few snowboarders on the slopes, skiers had cut two deep ruts under the T-bars making ascents difficult on a board. Frustrated by repeatedly falling over on the lift run I resorted to lying on my back with legs in the air being dragged backwards up the slope behind the metal bar! With limited kit hire available I had jeans on and cotton kiwifruit picking gloves, so before long my totally inappropriate clothing was saturated and I started to freeze.

By the time my minibus left, I was shivering so violently I couldn't hold a cup of coffee without shaking it over myself. My hands were frozen to the core, and that night woke me in agony. By morning they still felt numb and icy inside, so I visited a doctor who informed me I'd got frostnip and was lucky not to have frostbite! He gave me blood thinning tablets to get the circulation going again, but it would be many weeks before my fingers felt normal again.

FROM CHRISTCHURCH, I arranged another farm stay on a sheep station and hitchhiked out there. Stony Croft Farm sat on the flat expanse of the Canterbury Plains, backdropped in the distance by the snow-covered Southern Alps. Home to Sharon, Don, their two kids and two thousand odd sheep.

Lambing season had started, so I settled straight into farm routine of lamb patrol three times a day. Looking out for lost ones we drove grassy paddocks, separating new mothers from the mob and watching for problems. Often we chased down ewes with stuck heads of half-born lambs hanging out. It was a race against time to stop the lambs dying by strangulation.

Lost lambs were kept aside and hand fed until they could be paired with new mums, which sometimes meant skinning a dead lamb and tying that to a lost one. Gangly lambs sporting sheepskin coats tied on with bailing twine were a comical and ironic sight, but it often worked in tricking the ewe into thinking it was hers!

The dainty little lambs looked less happy on tailing day when hundreds got a needle jab, notches clipped from ears, tight rubber rings around nut sacks and their tails docked with a sharp hot iron. It was reminiscent of the sword fight scene in Life of Brian with blood squirting in jets from the freshly cut tail, accompanied by the acrid smell of burnt flesh!

With a powerful Honda quad bike to patrol and play on life on the farm seemed idyllic but I couldn't stay forever, so after two weeks bade farewell to the family, stuck my thumb out again and hitched north to Kaikoura.

LIKE MUCH OF South Island, the scenery around Kaikoura is rugged, untamed and spectacular, with snow-capped mountains meeting the chilly waters of the Pacific. Ocean currents collide just off the coast and the deep continental shelf runs close to the shore, creating rich waters for sperm whales.

I joined a small group and spent a morning aboard a fast RIB searching for the giant mammals. Our skipper powered the boat a mile offshore, killed the twin outboards and lowered a sonar microphone over the side. Everyone was silent with breaths held in anticipation of hearing telltale ticking sounds. We picked up a trace, found the direction and sped off, radioing sister Nature Watch boats to help locate the elusive whale. For ten minutes we cruised back and forth with all eyes scanning until a shout went out of "There she blows!"

Our captain edged close enough to smell its foul fishy breath. Moments later the massive mammals back arched, the tail rose and the fifty-footers flukes slipped beneath the surface. With waters plunging to 4000 feet it was unlikely we would see the Sperm whale again, so shot off in search of more goliaths.

Rough weather the previous day resulted in cancelled trips, but now the winds had dropped leaving dark, silky waters, perfect for dolphin and seal spotting as well as for whales. Five rare Hectors dolphin raced up to investigate our boat, and as we neared the coastline a colony of seals and pups put on a show as they played in swell sweeping around their rocky home.

After a tough hike up Mt Fyffe in snow, and many hours beachcombing and exploring the wild, beautiful Kaikoura peninsula, I left the scenic town behind and continued to hitch north.

Back on the North Island

WITHIN DAYS I had recrossed the Cook Strait, hitched north from Wellington and reached Ohakune, home of The Big Carrot. From here I'd hoped to hike Tongariro National Park but found it closed, due to a thick blanket of snow. Instead, I had to content myself with the spectacular sight of snow-covered Mt Ruapehu volcano and the seven and a half metre tall carrot! The carrot, allegedly the world's largest, was made for a tv commercial, and now stands at the roadside as Ohakune grows most of the North Islands crop in the regions rich volcanic soils.

I carried on north to Taupo hoping to do a tandem skydive, but when I arrived in town, the skies were too cloudy to jump. Days later the weather still hadn't improved, so arranged yet another farm stay. After a year of backpacking, surviving on budget meals, the best thing about farm stays was often their food. At Tokoroa equestrian farm, I had free access to all grub cupboards, prompting complaints from the groom who did the shopping. I hate it when backpackers come here to work, she said, because our cupboards always get stripped bare. That's why we do farm stays! I replied with a grin.

WHEN THE SKIES cleared over Taupo I set straight off for its tiny airport where I traded my dollars for a jumpsuit and harness. I was given a worryingly brief two-minute training course, and moments later our light aircraft lifted off!

Circling higher spectacular views distracted me with snow-capped volcanoes and the lakes brilliant blue tones, but I snapped back to reality when the jumpmaster told me to get ready.

As we neared the drop zone, I strapped on my helmet, donned goggles and gloves and shuffled across the floor. Mark clipped in behind me then slid open the door. Roaring air instantly drowned out the engine. Nine thousand feet below green grass covered the ground. It looked further.

I edged forward, hung both feet into the void, and checked my harness clips for the tenth time. Mark told me to push my head back, hook thumbs beneath the harness and remember to arch my back.

Moments later he pushed, and we plummeted from

the plane. Accelerating toward Earth seconds disappeared in intense sensory overload. Blasting air buffeted my body and assaulted my ears as we hurtled down. Within moments we were falling at 200 kph.

A gloved thumb appeared in front of my goggles, the signal for free-fall position and I stretched wide into a star shape. Far below the tiny shapes of airport buildings almost disappeared next to Taupo's urban sprawl.

As gravity sped us unerringly towards ground, the mind-blowing thought struck that our unopened parachute was effectively untested! Then seconds later webbing straps wrenched into my shoulders and groin with too much force as Mark pulled the ripcord. The chute had opened!

In just 30 seconds we had fallen six thousand feet!

Our pace changed, and we drifted peacefully down the final 3000 feet, gazing down on tiny vehicles moving on roads stretching for miles and minuscule dots that gradually grew into people.

Below, everything looked odd viewed through dangling legs and as we crossed the airstrip a small plane took off beneath my feet. Mark threw the canopy into some stomach-churning turns and moments later we landed in the grass.

Back on the ground, I was still buzzing with adrenaline and the wide grin I wore stayed with me for the rest of the day. Like my bungy jumps it was over too fast and I wanted to fly then fall out of the plane again. After such an intense rush it's hard to return to normality, and I spent the afternoon reliving my jump gazing up at the sky!

FOR A FINAL kiwi adventure, I hitchhiked to Waitomo, to try Black Water Rafting.

The trip started in a car park where wetsuits and inflated truck inner tubes were handed out before hiking through dripping rainforest to a cave entrance. One by one we clambered down into darkness followed by two guides, who took great delight in telling us of all the nasties lurking inside. Their story about finger-eating eels was easy to ignore, but I wasn't keen on large cricket-like insects landing on my face in the dark!

Despite the horror stories I set off at the front with just a dim glow from my headlight barely penetrating the gloom. As I edged through waist deep waters meandering into the unknown, the kiwi guides bringing up the rear kindly provided a constant wind up commentary intended to scare!

Soon the cave constricted, forcing us to crawl on bellies before emerging below a refreshing subterranean waterfall, then as the water deepened, and we floated along on the tubes. Linking tubes with our feet we formed a human chain, turned off head torches and glided sedately through pitch-black tunnels. It was a strange sensation drifting in silence through the snaking river-cave accompanied only by the soft sound of lapping water. Above our heads, hundreds of tiny glowworms lit the cave roof like an astral display.

This time I'd chosen to go right at the back, so when the chain separated I drifted alone in darkness, and the feeling of solitude was absolute. With zero light penetrating the cave it was pitch black, but still possible to sense the walls looming presence and shoot out a hand to prevent head meeting rock.

All too soon I glimpsed daylight ahead, re-emerged into the world and drifted downstream to a waiting minibus. After hot showers, we warmed further with steaming bowls of pumpkin soup and stacks of thick butter-laden toast.

MY TIME IN New Zealand was drawing to an end, but just before leaving Auckland I had some important paperwork to complete and slipped a rather cheeky application for a tax refund into the post.

… Well, it had to be worth a try!

South East Asia
1992

Kelimutu: Lost and Alone on a Volcano.

THE IMMIGRATION OFFICIAL did not look happy. His expression told me in an instant my excuse wouldn't wash. It appeared that my three-month holiday visa had expired, and apparently I had overstayed my welcome by 14 weeks, so I'd broken the law!

An easy mistake to make, I'd claimed, as I had been travelling so long and had little reason, or need, to know the day of the week, let alone the date! Anyway, I was departing the country, so what could they do? Kick me out!!

Leaving Australia after 18 months exploring the land down under and neighbouring New Zealand, I still didn't want to go home, so decided to take a slow route back overland. Indonesia's many islands looked appealing for more adventure, and from Darwin, it was a short, inexpensive hop over to Timor aboard Ansett Airlines. So after a stern talking to and a passport seen stamp added to my collection, I climbed boarding steps and waved the country goodbye.

Touchdown at Kupang International Airport, which amounted to one small building, two planes, and a short airstrip, was to be the start of four months island hopping vaguely heading towards home.

Asia came as quite a culture shock and a stark contrast to anything I'd seen or experienced before. The poverty and squalor looked appalling, with primitive shacks supporting thatched palm or rusty tin roofs. Narrow muddy tracks running wild with livestock and scruffy toddlers separated the jumbled collections of huts crowded together. Pigs foraged a sprawling rubbish dump spread across the beach. Yet everywhere friendly smiling faces called out "Hello Mr! Where you from?" or sometimes even "Hello Mrs! Where you go?"

A group of us who'd met an hour earlier on the plane arrived at a hostel in search of rooms, but the hostess seemed surprised at our reluctance to share the solitary, communal bed platform proudly offered.

"What, no jiggy-jiggy?"

The five of us moved on…

AFTER A FEW days in Kupang we decided to cross over to the island of Flores, so we squeezed inside 'Sindi Loper', along with far too many locals, and the brightly painted bemo taxi sped us towards the ferry terminal. A crazy, erratic ride ensued as our driver slalomed through swarming bemos with one hand on the horn, and music pumping full volume from massive under seat speakers. Like ours, many had pop star names and before we reached port, we passed both Mick Jagger and Madonna on the road.

The ferry to Larantuka was due to leave at two, but we had to board three hours earlier, which seemed way too early but at least allowed us to find seats. As we waited more and more people boarded and our boat became ever more crowded. Every scrap of deck space was taken. Bodies and luggage were wedged everywhere. Some even laying underneath lorries or atop their tarpaulins.

Departure time came and still we waited in the sweltering heat. After four sweaty dreary hours on the dangerously overloaded ferry, a sudden mad exodus started to a boat moored alongside and the fight was on for seats. Passengers frantically clambered from upper deck windows, stretching across to the other boat, whilst others lobbed bags and provisions over the gap!

By the time we pushed our way on board only floor space remained so with backpacks for pillows we settled in for a long, cramped, overnight crossing. Eight hours after first boarding the new ferry left at last, finally arriving in Larantuka mid morning.

FROM LARANTUKA TO Labuan Bajo, a single dirt road ran across Flores, and buses, like tarmac, were limited, and always overloaded. The first had seats for nineteen, yet somehow thirty people were packed inside. Three more hung from the open door. Others clung to luggage piled on the roof and a rear ladder provided a precarious perch for yet more. One journey took over six hours to cover a mere 100 kilometres. Five times we stopped to fix punctures, but the atrocious state of the island's roads and its treacherous bridges were mainly to blame.

Bridges had been formed from two bearers with just loose sheets of steel and logs lying on top. To reduce his load sometimes the driver would let passengers walk across, but usually, it was a case of being ready to climb out of a window if the bridge collapsed!

Fallen trees and rock-slides provided further hazards along with huge sections where the rough track had been washed away by floods. Several times we had near head-on collisions with equally overloaded buses. Brake pads were probably expensive here but copious use of the horn was free, so why bother slowing for blind bends!

In an attempt to maintain macho images, some drivers recklessly sped through villages to prove bravado. Wearing mirror shades and cool expressions sometimes t-shirt choice undermined their efforts. With a fashion for anything written in English, one young driver sported a sparkly number with I'm A Little Princess emblazoned on the front!

Aside from the five of us, chain-smoking locals filled the small bus taking their produce to market, including a gaggle of scrawny chickens intent on escape and one grumpy trussed up pig! Our bus was old and tired, the heat stifling and the clove cigarette smoke cloying. So punctures came as a welcome relief, giving a chance to get backpacks off laps, unfurl cramped limbs and enjoy beautiful scenery out in fresh air.

Flores is indescribably green with acres of towering

palms crowding its shores, and hillsides lined with hundreds of rice paddies carved out by past generations, still worked by hand and ever-present water-buffalo. Sporadically, isolated communities interrupted the verdant scenery. Balancing bulging sacks or baskets on heads black-haired women unhurriedly strolled mid-street. Naked toddlers chased squealing micro pigs. Bamboo and palm huts blended naturally into their background. Fleeting glimpses and snapshots of simple rural lives.

A GENTLE, POLITE but insistent rapping on my door roused me moments before four. It felt much too early to get up. But fifteen minutes later I clambered aboard an open-sided truck fitted out with rows of wooden bench seats and started an hour-long ascent up Mount Kelimutu.

It was a slow gruelling slog. With gears grinding and transmission whining, the ageing truck lurched and rattled its way up the steep winding track. Roadside glowworms illuminated our route in the gloom aided by dozens of darting fireflies. When at last the tired truck made it to the summit, it dropped us and drove back to the village, leaving our group to await sunrise and make the three-hour return walk down to Moni village.

As the first rays crept over the horizon we got a glimpse of the spectacle before us. Hundreds of feet below lay a huge lake encircled by sheer-sided volcanic cone. Beyond the jagged crater rugged terrain dropped dramatically away to the coast. When the orb of the rising sun broke free from cloud cover, the scene flooded with warmth and colour revealing the full magnitude of Kelimutu.

Below us lay three crater lakes, each one a different colour. The first an unnatural, milky shade of vivid turquoise, lay alongside a second black lake which nobody had noticed due to its water being so dark. Behind our vantage point, the third was the colour of Coke, green-tinged around its edges. Two weeks earlier this lake had been pure white.

Triggered by volcanic gas activity the lakes periodically change colour and have been known to do so six times in a single year. Although Kelimutu last erupted in 1968, much is still going on beneath the surface.

After a while, most of the group started to drift towards the track leading to the village. But I wanted to explore further so headed off alone in the opposite direction hoping to link with the road from the far side of the crater.

My route along the rim was spectacular and afforded some of the best views of the coloured lakes and their plunging, stratified sides. Looking out over the sleeping volcano I felt to be on top of the world with Flores verdant jungle spread beneath me. A lush panoramic vista that stretched down to the sea on either side of the narrow island.

I met a Swiss couple who'd turned back on the trail, and in hindsight, that's what I should have done, but instead headed for the next peak along a perilous knife-edged ridge. Later, when I passed a rough wooden cross marking where someone had fallen to their death, I should have taken it as a sign and retraced my steps, but kept moving and left the harrowing spot behind.

Before long the narrow trail petered out forcing me to backtrack and follow another vague path heading down. A few minutes earlier I'd heard voices below so felt confident the road must be close and carried on. But now the route was becoming increasingly hazardous, forcing me to slide on all fours down dried up rain gullies. Then I reached a wall of impenetrable jungle.

I'd been hiking for an hour so didn't want to turn back and was convinced the road must be close so forced my way in. Using chest and shoulders I rammed through thick undergrowth, shielding my face with both arms. The vegetation was so dense I could barely see three metres ahead and deep ground foliage meant I couldn't see where I placed my feet. Tangled roots and concealed rocks littered the steep terrain, and I fell several times, crashing down through greenery.

More and more vegetation got wrapped around me, forcing stops to roll over the accumulated mass in order to continue. It was slow going, exhausting and becoming increasingly perilous.

A thin t-shirt gave scant protection so my arms were getting shredded by sharp branches and spiky plants. Worries and doubts about finding the road crowded my mind, but I was fully committed having fallen down two near-vertical slopes which would be impossible to climb back up.

The hasty pre-dawn departure meant I'd left my water bottle behind and I badly needed some fluids. Thoughts of poisonous snakes, spiders and malarial mosquitoes started to play on my mind.

Desperately hoping the road must be close I kept forcing my way down, all too aware that if I fell and broke an ankle, I probably wouldn't be found for at least a day. My group was the only one visiting Kelimutu today, and several hours had passed since I left them, so most would be nearing Moni by now. Nobody else would visit the volcano until dawn tomorrow at the earliest…

For all I knew the road may have been off to the right and I could be moving away from it. A worrying and very real possibility. Having no horizon and a limited field of vision made orientation difficult. I could do little but follow the slope.

As I crashed onwards feeling battered and very alone, and the road continued to elude me, the serious nature of my predicament started to get to me, and I battled to stay calm and keep a clear head. The treacherous terrain had already taken its toll and there was a real danger of seriously injuring myself. I was probably the last person on the volcano and knew I wouldn't be missed until nightfall.

Just when panic was creeping in, I had my first piece of luck. I heard a truck and thought it sounded close.

Hope returned and kept me heading down. Much later I would learn the truck had been the only other vehicle on Kelimutu that day.

Suddenly a branch whipped across my face scratching out a contact lens, so now I couldn't see clearly! I couldn't push it back into place so kept moving until I remembered a tiny mirror inside my daypack. Thinking the dislodged lens would be in my eye, I was shocked to see it on the bridge of my nose. Sweat and dirt had stuck it there and by a small miracle, I stopped before it had fallen. Relieved to have full vision again I pushed on, but still couldn't see the road. Trees surrounded me which could have provided vantage points, but all were too wide or too slippery to climb.

With increasing desperation, I clambered into a gully with a stream, thinking I could follow the watercourse out, but abandoned the idea when it went off at a tangent and scrambled back up the other side.

I ploughed ahead, but this time a steep drop far too risky to descend forced a backtrack, so again I followed the stream, sloshing through water and adding soaked trainers to my misery. I thought the nightmare ordeal couldn't get any worse, but then the gully ended with a 40-foot waterfall, forcing yet another change of course.

Increasingly stressed and physically exhausted I stumbled on, constantly tripping and falling, being punished by rocks and branches, really struggling to remain calm. But then there it was, at last, the road! What a wonderful welcome sight. The relief was immense.

But my troubles weren't over as the road was a hundred feet straight below me with no route down in sight.

I then had a final piece of luck... I heard voices!

Crouching low and peering down, I could just see the Swiss couple, Jean and Sandra, walking down the dirt road. Seconds later and I would have missed them. Other than me they were probably the only people on Kelimutu. I felt so relieved to see them. I shouted to stop them, but they couldn't see me. At last, they spotted me. And saw my predicament.

To my left, a rocky slope plunged at the road, to the right it didn't look much better. We had little communication as neither spoke English, but Jean pointed to my right. Damp, treacherous rock lined the cliff edge so again I forced my way back into the jungle, skirted further along and emerged still way above the road. Thick vegetation obscured the slope, giving me little visibility of a route down, but with hand signals, Jean indicated nowhere looked any better. The height and incline looked horrendous, but I had no choice other than attempt it.

Stepping forward, I fell almost immediately, crashing through thick foliage for thirty feet or more until I stopped, legs dangling mid-air. A tangled mass of vegetation had prevented me from falling further. Now there really was no turning back. Carefully I extracted myself and with little control continued to plunge and slide, smashing through everything in my path. As I staggered out of the undergrowth at the foot of the slope Jean took my photograph.

Incredibly, I survived the fall without breaking bones but was in a sorry state otherwise. Without the sheer luck of catching my new friends, the outcome could have been very different, and it turned out they were the last people on Kelimutu that day.

Three long hours later I arrived shattered at the hostel in Moni. Battered, bruised, emotionally drained and covered in cuts and scratches. My ripped clothes were filthy, and I was longing for a shower, but it would be many more hours before I dragged myself fully clothed into the cubicle as the water tank had run dry!

Instead, I had a slow wait for afternoon rains to refill the tank, whilst I told and retold the story a dozen times as other backpackers wandered in, saw the state I was in and said: "Shit! What the hell happened to you?"

Here be Dragons

A PITIFUL BLEAT escaped the lips of the goat. The animal suddenly seemed reluctant to go much further, yet moments before had been scampering merrily in front. Now the guide was having to drag it along by its rope lead. The poor goat was agitated and clearly distressed.

Perhaps it had something to do with a large wooden sign we'd just passed on the wide forest trail. The sign which read: Dangerous Area. Watch Out Komodos Crossing. Be Silent!

EARLY THE PREVIOUS morning I'd boarded a small boat in Labuan Bajo, Flores, along with Naomi and a few backpackers for a three-day cruise around Rinca and Komodo Islands, ending at Sumbawa.

The trip sounded idyllic but got off to a bad start when the boatman claimed to know nothing of our booking. We marched back to the hostel, found Amir, who we'd paid in full, and made him come to the harbour. After a heated exchange, it seemed there weren't enough people to fill the boat, so Amir took us to find Agus. He took us to a new boat, took more money from us and then took off, never to be seen again!

The cruiser was, in reality, a dilapidated wooden

vessel with little space for its few passengers, but at least it floated and appeared to have an engine! Boarding was risky as we had to be ferried out on a low-slung dugout canoe. With the extra weight of two Westerners and two large backpacks, the waterline was inches from engulfing the tiny craft!

A ten-foot-long tarp covered deck with a cramped wheelhouse for the skipper and a raised open-topped sleeping platform at the rear would be home for the next three days. The short platform was just big enough for two and located right above the engine room and 'Lavatroy', which consisted of two planks and a gap, but not quite the headroom to stand!

Following untamed coastline we motored south through clear glassy waters towards Rinca Island, stopping en route to snorkel in the rich warm Flores Sea. Arriving at Rinca, unsurprisingly, there was no sign of Agus, but instead we were greeted by another guide who wanted paying again. So once more several thousand rupiahs changed hands before our new so-called guide led us on a short, silent loop around the rocky island.

Rinca has a small population of Dragons, but none were spotted, just a handful of wild horses and the odd dozy, grazing water-buffalo. As we neared the boat a playful troop of grey monkeys showing off in trees above our heads made the hike worth the effort in the heat.

Back aboard, our skipper coaxed the ageing engine into life once more and motored off towards Komodo Island, home of the fearsome Dragons. Chugging past rocky uninhabited islands as the horizon swallowed the sun, the skies filled with tens of thousands of flying foxes winging their way to feeding grounds.

Dawn found us lying at anchor just off a sandy beach in Liang Bay with not a soul in sight. A solitary boat tied up to the tall jetty and a simple hut on the shore were the only signs of life. It was a scene of total tranquillity. But just a few short hours later that feeling of serenity would be shattered as I watched a violent scrum of Komodo Dragons rip a goat to shreds before devouring it.

SOON AFTER PASSING the warning sign, a huge Dragon lumbered out of the undergrowth towards us, it's long forked tongue flicking. Immediately, a guide headed it off using all his weight on a lengthy wooden crook pushed into the neck of the beast. Humans aren't usually on the menu for the massive reptiles, but they are opportunistic carnivorous predators, possessing surprising speed and over the years a few people have been killed. One unlucky German tourist disappeared on the island almost without trace. All that was found of him was a camera and his hat...

After our first encounter, several people made panicked sprints when more Komodos appeared at intervals along the unfenced trail. Eventually, we came to a small staked off enclosure in the woods, inside was little more than information boards, but it was right next to a large feeding pit! With a swift throat slit, the jittery goat was sacrificed and hurled down into the pit.

In seconds waiting Dragons were on the warm body fighting for food. Fanned around the goat ten huge reptiles tore its carcass to pieces in a scrum-like tug-of-war, standing on each other as they jostled to sink teeth into flesh. With Dragons devouring large chunks soon little evidence remained of the poor animal.

With the free offering finished several Dragons turned their attention to the tourists, scrambling up steep banks from the pit towards us. Their taste for blood had not been sated. The wooden posts surrounding us had seemed sturdy enough but witnessing the power of the eight-foot monsters made me start to doubt that. Also, at some point, we had to leave the enclosure to hike back…

Now just feet away, I could see the savage claws that made short work of shredding the goat and wide jaws lined with dozens of raked-back teeth still dripping red saliva. With armour-scaled skins, cold reptilian eyes and long yellow forked tongues, Komodo Dragons truly look the prehistoric monsters they are.

WEIGHING UP TO ninety kilos and growing to ten feet, Komodo Dragons are powerful predators. They live on deer and carrion but sometimes take larger prey. Their bite contains toxins and anticoagulant that will, in time, kill bigger animals unlucky enough to be ambushed or attacked. When a water buffalo is killed, its carcass will soon be stripped as they can consume eighty percent of their body weight at one sitting. Dragons also display cannibalistic behaviour and will eat baby Komodos given the chance, so youngsters live up trees for the first few years of their lives.

Komodo Dragons are members of the monitor lizard family and are believed to be a relict population of a giant species once widespread through Australia and Indonesia. Fossil remains similar to Dragons have been found in Australia, dating back over three million years. But now, aside from Komodo and Rinca, they only exist in small pockets on a handful of neighbouring islands. Normally they don't pose a threat to human populations living nearby, however, they do cause occasional outrage with their disturbing habit of digging up the dead!

WHEN ACTIVITY IN the feeding pit settled down our guides deemed it safe to return to the boats. The walk passed without incident, but back at the harbour, we discovered our skipper had disappeared abandoning us on the island.

The other boat skipper was, of course, ready to take more of our money, and with over two thousand Dragons living on the small island, staying any longer didn't seem a sensible option. So once again we parted with more cash.

Soon we were Sumbawa bound, aboard another ancient vessel just as slow and noisy as the previous one. The skipper stopped later for more snorkelling, but everyone seemed reluctant to dive in now we knew that Dragons were strong swimmers!

Just as we neared dock in Sape, the boat's steering

broke leaving the captain with no control over his craft. It was beginning to look like we would need a fourth boat to complete the trip until the mate managed to get a line ashore and pulled us in.

It seemed a fitting end to the somewhat farcical trip, as besides the boat changes, somehow a whole day had disappeared from the cruise and we had paid several times over just to continue.

But the cost of visiting the fearsome Dragons of Komodo Island was nothing compared to the price paid by the German tourist.

China
1992

Into The People's Republic of China

SECONDS BEFORE TOUCHDOWN I glanced sideways into kitchens and living rooms of tower blocks lining the runway at Hong Kong's notorious Kai Tak airport, ranked amongst the world's most dangerous. Descending into the concrete and glass corridor squeezed amidst the cities skyscraper forest it seemed the aircraft's wingtip would almost graze apartment windows. I couldn't decide whether the landing was more scary for passengers, pilot or the tens of thousands of people living below!

From the confined airport I headed for downtown Kowloon and found a room on the sixteenth floor in Chungking Mansions, but the overcrowded tower block seemed more dump than mansion. A seedy, maze-like shopping arcade occupied the ground floor, full of Chinese and Indians trading from tiny spaces hemmed together in a chaotic mass. Small, slow lifts allegedly served the large building, but when they were working, waiting times could be fifteen minutes or more. Taking the stairs wasn't a good idea either as I soon discovered. Piss stains and piles of rubbish spread down the stone steps, which were home to rats, drunks and deals of a dubious nature.

Eight bunks had somehow been squeezed into my room but left little space to stand in the humid, airless dorm. In over twenty months on the road, it was the worst hostel by far. But whilst staying there I bumped into Casper, a Danish backpacker also heading for China, and we decided to travel there together.

Leaving the squalor of Chungking behind we threaded through busy streets to the Chinese Embassy and ninety Hong Kong dollars later departed with fresh visa stamps. A bus took us to Hung Hom and from there caught a train to the border at Lo Wu.

It was an easy departure to make, and I was glad to leave the dismal Mansions behind. Four days in the crowded city was enough for me, and I longed for some real food after reluctantly living on McDonald's, due to high prices elsewhere. With Hong Kong being the gateway to China, the main purpose of the visit was to get a visa and book my ticket aboard the Trans Mongolian railway.

Just ten years earlier The People's Republic of China had been completely closed to independent foreign travellers and having heard tales of problems encountered by other backpackers, I expected difficulties at the border. But after filling out countless official forms, we simply strolled into China.

Signs immediately changed to ones written in Hanzi. Tens of thousands of these Chinese characters exist, and the challenges of travel instantly took on a whole new dimension. We wanted to catch a bus to Canton, but failed at the first hurdle because of indecipherable signs, and caught a train instead as the station was easier to find! Two hours later the crowded train eased to a stop, and we spilled onto the platform amongst countless Chinese. Aside from Casper, there wasn't a single Westerner in sight!

Soon taxi touts spotted us, so again we took the easy option. We needed to get to Shamian Island, but the touts wanted an outrageous fare of 150 F.E.C's. When we got the cost down to ten, we agreed and followed the tout to a cab.

As we climbed into the car, a uniformed official snatched the taxi license from its holder on the dash and stalked off with it. Shouting, the angry cabby drove after him, leapt out and both disappeared inside a building. Ten minutes later the irate driver returned and drove us fast to the hostel and then followed us inside. With the hostel owner translating, it transpired the driver had been fined for being a 'bad man' and wanted me to sign a note stating he had been helpful and honest. With that, he hoped he would get his license back!

Heading for Qingping market next morning I got ripped off by money changers whose slick tactics and quick hands resulted in me losing some cash. I expected to get cheated, so watched them closely, but they were too good and distracted us constantly as notes changed hands.

Stalls offering a massive array of dried animal parts used in traditional Chinese medicine filled the sprawling street market. Deer antlers, hooves, leg bones, seahorses, coiled snakes, stretched lizards and long dark tongues lined the trestles, amongst no end of unidentifiable body parts. In the live market, we found a depressing selection of sad looking animals stuffed into cages, ready to be sold for the plate. Cramped wire prisons trapped cats, dogs, deer, hedgehogs, tortoises, a mongoose and many other mammals in poor condition. It was a sickening sight, particularly the conditions they were kept in, but worse was to come when we noticed a skinned live rabbit lying gasping on a butcher's block.

Later that evening, despite the day's sights, I tried the local speciality of snake, displayed writhing in large glass tanks so diners could choose which they ate. An eyeball arrived at the table with my deep-fried snake, and a second dish came served complete with the chicken's neck, head and beak! As I worked my way through the chewy snake which tasted a little like the chicken, its accusatory eyeball seemed to stare up at me with contempt.

Amongst the restaurants more usual dishes, the menu card tempted diners with delights such as cat, fur seal and even turtle. But the following day I found another offering boiled goose intestines and organs and no longer felt the need to eat!

FROM CANTON, OUR next destination was Yangshuo,

which entailed a long ferry ride up the Pearl River to Wuzhou. Having survived three days aboard a packed Indonesian ferry where my stale, sweltering, windowless cabin held over a hundred passengers, and each sleeping platform was shared by ten, I thought the overnighter to Wuzhou would to be more pleasant, despite the bargain price.

I was wrong and my quarters for the next twenty hours was a simple wooden slot six feet long by two feet wide. Separated from fellow passengers only by a slim, six-inch-high divider to either side, thirty-five people slept sardine fashion in a line. Below my cot, the second run of sleeping slots had barely the headroom to sit up. Filling the space between mirror-image bunks on the opposite side of the boat were deckchairs, the economy class. We had paid extra for a sleeper upgrade and even got grubby paper-thin reed mats to lie on!

Life aboard the battery farm liner soon became a cycle of playing cards, visiting the bar or lying wedged atop the unpadded planks of my communal bed. Hours dragged as slowly as the old boat's progress upstream through thick brown waters. Outside a flat, rural landscape was rendered even less interesting by dull grey skies obscuring much of the view.

A Chinese passenger celebrating his 18th birthday invited us over as guests of honour, even giving the first cuts from a candle-topped cake to us. The young students seemed keen to practice English with the rare foreigners on board.

Out on the busy river, a procession of primitive boats with patchwork hulls passed by. Filthy, fume-belching tugs laboured past pulling convoys of low-slung coal-laden barges, whilst hopeful fisherman lowered pivoting nets from muddy banks into the murky waters below.

DOCKING NEXT DAY in Wuzhou, a bus was waiting, but it wasn't long before the vehicle was brought to a premature halt. There had been an accident involving a truck and a horse-drawn cart, and my eyes met the gruesome sight of the poor animal being butchered by the roadside where it lay in the mud.

Ten long, uncomfortable hours later the dilapidated bus reached its destination. After Canton's filthy, crowded, chaotic streets Yangshuo's quiet roads came as a complete contrast. Nestled beneath spectacular jutting karst scenery on the banks of the meandering river Li, the small town seemed friendly and was an unbelievably cheap place to stay. A basic hotel room set me back seventy pence a night and a few doors away, Lisa's place served big plates of delicious food for as little as thirty.

Lisa's soon turned into our local, but visits all too easily led to bad hangovers as a large beer was half the price of bottled water! Backpackers always filled the small cafe and many had been in town for some time, but with beer costing so little, that came as no great surprise!

HIRING BIKES WE set out for Moon Hill, and once out of town, the idyllic rural landscape looked almost un-touched by time. Aside from the odd laden cart being hand pulled back from the fields, the roads were devoid of vehicles. Lush rice paddies lined roadsides, worked by water buffalo and farmers clad in communist blue beneath conical straw hats. Rugged karsts rose like jagged teeth behind the peaceful paddies and stretched far into the distance.

Recognising Moon Hill by a huge semicircular hole through its limestone, we left our bikes at the bottom and started the steep climb. With not a soul in sight, we thought we'd have the summit to ourselves until we heard voices and our arrival was met with calls of "Hello Coca-Cola! Hello?"

Earlier, in the middle of nowhere, we passed the surreal sight of a solitary fridge standing beneath a tree at the roadside. The tall fridge was manned by two females selling drinks and we'd ignored the same call, but now sweating on the summit, the cold Coke seemed worth the extortionate price extracted by the entrepreneurial girls squatting beside their cool box.

From the top of Moon Hill, a jigsaw-like mosaic of paddy fields spread below with a broad placid river snaking through the middle. Ancient encircling karsts, formed millennia ago by rainwater erosion, melted moodily into distance amidst the low-lying mist.

WITH BIKE HIRE costing as little as the beer, we spent days exploring dirt tracks and discovering tucked-away rustic villages. Several times as we approached small children screamed and ran away, and it was clear they had never seen Westerners before! Casper being tall and blonde must have appeared even more alien and scary to them. Wherever we went we always attracted great interest, and many people simply stopped in their tracks and stared.

CLIMBING DOWN INTO the dank stillness of Black Buddha Water Cave, we spent three hours exploring underground. With only dim torches to illuminate our way, four of us followed the guide Chunsheng into blackness. With so little light and no useful communication coming from Chung, we felt like pioneers as we explored the winding complex of caverns. Descending a bamboo ladder Paul had a moment of panic when a rung broke plunging him into the black void below. Luckily he landed almost unscathed, but the episode did little to encourage his reluctant girlfriend to venture much further!

Feeling our way by foot we inched through chilly chest deep water clinging to rocks for support. Sometimes the walls closed in forcing us to squeeze through tight gaps in the slippery rock. In other places, gaping dry caverns were home to alien formations and agitated colonies of bats disturbed by our presence. When at last we emerged muddy and soaked into daylight, everyone was more than ready to head back to Lisa's for bowls of Mongolian beef and bottles of LiQuan beer.

After nine lazy, tranquil days in town, little remained on Lisa's menu we hadn't tasted so it seemed like a good time to move on!

Our next stop would be Chengdu, a thousand miles northwest. A journey neither of us was looking forward to...

Ten Thousand Steps to Heaven: Climbing China's Holy Mountain

A SIX-HOUR EAR-SPLITTING, bone-rattling ride took us from Yangshuo to Luzhou, aboard a bus whose driver believed near-constant, aggressive use of the air horn to be better than the bother of using his brakes. From Luzhou bus terminal, a primitive tricycle-taxi pedalled us to the train station, with bums perched on rusty metal rails and the packs stuffed beneath our feet. The train ride to Chongqing was spent in the relative comfort of soft sleeper class whose bunks were stacked three high throughout the noisy open carriage. The short mattress provided just about space to wedge my backpack as a rather bulky pillow.

As the only Westerners aboard the packed carriage, we attracted plenty of attention with people constantly watching. I'd grown accustomed to this in other parts of Asia, but here it was hard to get a reaction when I smiled back, waved or said ni hao. Often the Chinese didn't even look away, they just continued to stare. Sometimes on the street, we'd been surrounded in moments by a crowd of staring faces when we stopped to look at something. I found it rude, and it became a daily challenge to crack a smile from the sea of deadpan faces.

Full-volume excitable babbling blaring from a speaker inches above my head awoke me in an instant at six the next morning. Someone had decided it was time all the passengers got up, and I hoped that perhaps we were nearing our destination. Sadly, we weren't even close, and the journey dragged on for 30 dreary hours, but even then we still had a lot further to go.

Chongqing station was absolutely chaotic and crushed amongst hordes of passengers crowded around the office we battled to sort out onward tickets. There had been a mix-up, and it seemed ours were for the next day, but spending the night on the cold platforms moulded plastic seats was not an option. Somehow, with minutes to spare, we secured the correct tickets to Chengdu.

Our hard seat class carriage had seats for 120 and they quickly filled, but more and more people kept pouring in. Bodies were everywhere and the heat and din soon became intolerable. Across tiny tables, low-backed, bolt-upright seats faced each other in pairs making sleep impossible unless you had the window to lean on. My knees touched the opposite passenger, and when I tried to stretch a leg out by pushing what I assumed to be luggage aside, a fist thumped my shin. Somebody had crawled beneath the seat to sleep!

By morning the stale carriage looked filthy with beer bottles, cigarette butts, food-scraps, and plastic cartons littering the floor, but a cleaner showed up and just swept the lot straight out of the door! Eleven long hours after boarding we left the train behind, took a minibus into the city, checked into a cheap hotel and at last got some sleep.

AFTER THE QUIET streets of Yangshuo, Chengdu came as another stark contrast, and the wide city streets teemed with thousands of cyclists. Beneath striped umbrellas, white-uniformed policemen stood on pedestals at busy junctions blowing whistles and waving, in a seemingly futile attempt to control the ceaseless flow of pedal traffic!

We booked into the Black Coffee Hotel, a converted bomb shelter with thick steel doors and no natural light, which was staffed by stern-faced ladies who strode the corridors at night clanking bunches of keys like sadistic jailers!

Leaving our underground cell behind, we crossed a bridge spanning the Jin river, past airgun punters shooting at balloons strung above the polluted water, and wandered towards the Flower Garden for breakfast. Passing the park with waltzing couples and old folk limbering up with tai chi, we spotted a solitary man wielding a long Samurai sword! But he attracted no attention other than from us.

Squatting sellers lined Chengdu's grubby pavements scraping a living from paltry selections of items spread at their feet, or polishing dusty shoes in exchange for a few yuan. Pockets of old men dressed in Communist blue huddled around card tables or played Chinese dominoes, smoking long pipes and spitting on the floor.

As we backtracked after breakfast a bloated pig brought excitement to the air-gunners as it floated downriver providing a brief change from boring balloons!

IN CANTON, I'D cashed the last of my traveller's cheques and was running low on funds, so urgently needed to find a bank, but they were few and far between. Chengdu, fortunately, had a branch of the Bank of China and I walked in prepared, with phrasebook and passport in hand. When my turn came at the counter, all work behind it ceased as every staff member stared at the rare Western specimen standing before them.

I handed over my credit card and passport along with a phrase book I'd underlined in places to make it clear what I wanted. First, my passport made its way slowly around the room, followed by my visa card. At each desk, the banker checked my photo, looked back at me, leafed through the passport, examined the plastic card, looked again at me, turned it over, passed it on, then resumed staring at me! My documents were scrutinised by every single person working for the bank, but nobody seemed to know what to do with them.

Whilst they travelled around the bank, the first cashier was writing and I realised he appeared to be translating something for me. Ten minutes later the passport and credit card finished their circuit and were handed back along with my phrase book and a short note which said: We Are Closed!

One hour later I departed with my money as I'd refused to leave and insisted they make the vital transaction. Whilst I waited the bank seemed a hive of inactivity and I watched idle, scruffy staff do little but sip tea from jam jars or fiddle with wooden abacuses.

The currency has become a daily annoyance, and every day black-market money changers call out "Hello change money" whenever they spot us. Officially, as tourists, we have to use Foreign Exchange Certificates (FEC's) which are the same value as yuan but in practice worth more. So most people want to be paid in FEC's but then give the change in yuan. Naturally, we want to use yuan whenever possible, so have to risk money changers on the street. Some places will take yuan, but many won't and insist on FEC's, whilst others don't seem to know what FEC's are! So just paying can be a daily battle. Having just spent two months in South East Asia, where even a bottle of water had to be haggled over, this has become wearing.

I heard a theory that FEC's were introduced by the government to prevent foreigners from becoming too friendly with Chinese folk, and if that's true the policy certainly worked!

STANDING ON THE edge of the eastern Himalayan highlands is Mount Emei, one of China's four sacred Buddhist mountains. Chengdu is relatively close to the holy mountain, yet to reach it we had to endure a crazy five-hour bus ride.

Our ageing bus was a typical battle-scarred death trap with bald tyres through to steel strand, steered by a driver with a death wish. The road was wide and straight allowing the bus to be driven fast, but hordes of cyclists crowded the road who displayed an utter disregard for their own safety. Our kamikaze driver wove recklessly around the unpredictable meandering riders at top speed using his air horn almost nonstop. With headphones on and music volume turned to maximum, it was still hard to endure the horn blasts. When we could take no more of the near-relentless racket we shouted "SHUT UP" in unison, which resulted only in a sea of faces turning to stare yet again at the strange foreigners.

Travelling through Asia you become accustomed to poor drivers and risky road behaviour but this driver was scary because the wide road allowed him to drive so fast. We had several near-collisions with oncoming trucks and I felt it was only a matter of time before he mowed down a cyclist or more.

The five-hour ride seemed much longer, but we escaped without injury, except for minor hearing damage, but then, were soon breathing noxious fumes belching from a two-stroke tuk-tuk exhaust. The toxic taxi dropped us in Baoguo, where we found a place to stay, dumped backpacks and went in search of food.

Baoguo was a tourist trap and vendors lined the street offering arrays of cheap shoddy gifts, such as chopsticks, figurines or vanity fans. Others sold more practical goods like maps and walking sticks, but further up the hill, we found stallholders with aphrodisiac potions and animal body parts.

Tiger's paws and bear claws were laid out on plastic sheets with monkey skulls and many unidentifiable pieces from other large mammals. Close by, old men kept chained monkeys imprisoned in tiny cages, hoping to charge ignorant tourists for cruel photos.

Later, we passed three infants lying abandoned by the roadside with a cardboard begging sign and a few crumpled yuan thrown at their feet. The toddler's parents were nowhere to be seen.

We found a restaurant but when our food arrived, the cooks came out to stare as we ate. The belching manager then sat down at our table and turned his back to watch the street. Meanwhile, a worker chose to mend a broken chair right behind me, whilst another stood manically grinning over our table pretending to box!

FOLLOWING BREAKFAST IN Baoguo we caught a bus to Wanniansi and began the ascent of Mt Emei a few minutes before ten. At first, the easy trail was packed with Chinese tourists making pilgrimages to the holy mountain but happily we left most behind at the first monastery we reached.

As the crowds thinned, and we ascended trails passing through lush forests of cedar and pine, we began to appreciate the tranquillity and natural beauty of the mountain. Walking up long flights of steps we climbed fragrant bamboo-lined corridors alive with birdsong.

The higher we climbed, the steeper the steps became and the more they tortured calf muscles. Endless steps ascended in straight runs until the top was glimpsed bringing hope of respite, but arrival at the brow was often met with the depressing sight of yet another daunting flight a short distance ahead.

We climbed steadily throughout the day, stopping to rest at ancient monasteries and temples along the way, but the grey stone steps were relentless. The first six hours were fine, but as physical and mental fatigue set in it got tougher. Our breaks became longer and more frequent and it didn't help motivation being passed by people who'd cheated and taken a bus halfway up the mountain. More demotivating still, were others coming down who indicated in hours how much further it was. And how hard it was!

We were taking a break when a team of porters laboured by. Bearing loads of forty bricks strapped to their backs and wearing open-toed sandals the sweating workers climbed past in slow procession, pausing only to hurl insults when I snapped a quick photo!

Later, a large aggressive monkey attacked us on the trail, forcing me to throw my daypack at it and run. But the unfazed creature started to rip the pack apart, so I ran back and booted the bag sending both it and the monkey flying. Luckily that worked, and it left us alone.

At five we reached the cable car station, and it was

tempting to take the easy option of a scenic ride up to the summit. Instead, we carried on and pushed hard for the top. To stay motivated I set myself a goal of six o'clock to reach the summit as someone told us it was maybe one or two hours away.

It was tough, relentless climbing and by the time I reached the top my head and heart were pounding and my face running with sweat. As I ran up the final short flight of steps, I got strange looks and must have been thought crazy by the Chinese pilgrims. I glanced again at my watch but had missed my goal by five minutes.

We'd made the 2500m ascent in a shade over eight hours, had hiked for almost 30 kilometres, and were standing on the summit at 3099m. But after climbing thousands of gruelling steps, there was nothing to see from the top as clouds had encircled the peak!

Despite it being summer there were still snow patches on the ground and feeling the cold we went to a hut and hired thick green military jackets. We booked into a draughty spartan room, then spent a freezing sleepless night lying fully clothed on lumpy beds. At five-thirty we ventured groggily out for sunrise and found the top crawling with green-coated Chinese tourists. The sun declined to put in even a brief appearance and cloud still enshrouded the summit obscuring all views, so we returned to our beds before taking the cable car down and a final bus off the mountain. Cold, tired and hungry we found a place selling food, wolfed down bowls of boiled rice and boarded a bus for Leshan.

Leshan is home to the Grand Buddha, which at 71 metres high is the largest and tallest in the world. His ears measure a massive seven metres from tip to lobe, and even his big toenail is almost two metres long! Carved from a sheer cliff face, the colossal figure faces towards holy Mt Emei and sits at the confluence of two rivers. It took ninety years to carve from solid rock, and the Buddha's monk creator died a few years before his life's work was finished. I thought the big Buddha looked a little bored, but that wasn't surprising as he has sat there for 1200 years!

In nearby Wulong Monastery, we found an impressive collection of painted life-size terracotta monks. One thousand statues depict long since passed monks who used to worship within the ancient monastery. Seated now in two rows around the walls, every face, expression, gesture and article of clothing was unique.

From Leshan we took a slower but much safer bus ride back to Chengdu, to buy onward tickets to Xian, home of the Terracotta Warriors, and spend another night locked in an underground cell at the Black Coffee Hotel. Guarded by grim-faced jailers!

Xian to Peking

ROCK AND HUNDREDS of tonnes of debris from a huge landslide had blocked the rail tracks according to the ticket office. Nobody knew how long it would take to clear or whether it would still be possible to reach Xian by train. Information was vague, so all we could do was hope and come back the next day. After weeks in China we had resigned ourselves to taking the easier, but expensive, route to buying tickets through state-run C.I.T.S. But even with them, it wasn't always straight-forward.

China International Travel Service had probably saved us a huge amount of hassle and as the staff were occasionally helpful, sometimes their service seemed worth the extra price paid! With so many languages and dialects spoken in China, even a phrase book was often of little help, and attempts to buy tickets at stations resulted in confusion, frustration or even desks abruptly closing, when the clerk decided it was too much hassle to help us!

Returning to C.I.T.S next day, surprisingly, they had two tickets for us but both aboard the dreaded hard seat class. With an expected duration of well over a day, assuming the track had actually been cleared, it was a daunting prospect and we tried to change our tickets at the station without success.

As usual, the train was stuffed to its seams and based on number of heads counted in our carriage I estimated two thousand people on board! It looked like we were in for another long grim journey until we chatted with the only other Westerner in sight. He planned to jump off at Ankan and continue by bus to Xian. With the uncertainty of the landslide situation it sounded like a better option, so after enduring fifteen long hours of hard seat hell we got off the train.

Trusting a bike bemo taxi to take us to the right bus station, we arrived just in time to grab front seats, a risky place to sit in Asia, but worth the gamble for extra legroom! We'd calculated the distance to be around 300 kilometres from a map and hoped for an optimistic five hours aboard the crowded bus. Six uncomfortable hours later I broke the cardinal rule and asked how much longer and was shown a spread hand. Five o'clock was an hour away, but when five pm passed and then six, realisation dawned that he meant five more hours!

It didn't help that our driver was saving fuel by cutting the engine whenever he could, then coasting down to a walking pace before he fired it up again! At least the landscape was stunning, and we wound through sheer-sided gorges and up precarious mountain passes which our erratic driver then attacked like rally stages!

Stopping to water roadside plants, I glanced up and noticed the roof luggage was moving and realised we had live cargo onboard. Ten large hessian sacks stuffed full of angry writhing snakes!

By the time the tired old workhorse finally pulled into Xian we had endured over twelve hours on the bus, but it would still be another two before we found beds for the night.

As usual, on exiting the bus a scrum of excitable touts surrounded us and the predictable pantomime ensued: Pull the phrase book out from my daypack, but instantly have it snatched from my hands. Grab it back from the ignorant tout, then run a finger under the translation for 'take me to the hotel' and point out which place in my guidebook. Get bombarded by loud incomprehensible responses from everyone jabbering at once, which soon attracts more touts who also join in. Lose patience with the fast-talking bickering touts, walk away, find some different touts and start the whole cycle again!

When a fare was finally agreed we squeezed into a motorbike trailer and were taken to the hotel. But not the right one! Eventually, our rider found the correct one, but it was too expensive, so we ended up catching yet another bus right across the city and at last found somewhere to stay. Our budget room was basic but had everything we needed after thirty hours without sleep; two beds and a door with a bolt!

IN 1974, FARMERS digging a well in fields at the foot of Lishan mountain to the east of Xian made a find that would lead to the discovery of the Terracotta Warriors.

When Qin Shi Huang Di, First Emperor of China, came to the throne, he commissioned the Terracotta Army to be constructed to protect him in his afterlife. Known as one of the great rulers, Qin unified the country and standardised economic, legal and political systems. But he also used slave labour to construct the Great Wall and his own immense burial tomb. After he died in 210 B.C, it's thought his son sealed the tomb with artisans and workers still inside. By burying them alive along with the Army, he ensured that the burial chambers location would remain secret!

Each of the 7000 Terracotta Warriors is a replica of a soldier who served in Qin's army, so every single one is individual and unique. The colossal burial complex covers an area of almost 38 square miles and also contains hundreds of terracotta horses and chariots, bronze figures and weapons.

Before leaving Xian we treated ourselves to a big Terracotta Warrior Breakfast, chosen from a rare menu translated into English, which was sadly only memorable because of its name. Usually, in restaurants, the only way to order was to wander between diners then motion the waiter over and point at dishes we wanted. It seemed rude but was preferable to starving!

We stocked up with snacks and boarded yet another train, bound this time for Beijing. Window seats would make hard seat class survivable, so we settled in for the long journey north and hoped it would be over in less than a full day.

Sitting opposite was a student who spoke English, and we'd been learning more about China when the young mother next to him suddenly became agitated. It turned out the student had just told her I came from England, so she thought I must have Aids! Apparently, propaganda had been stating that many Westerners, all Americans, and all English had the disease! I was appalled but at least it gave the chance to correct them. Through the student, we also learnt the Chinese thought of foreigners as being dirty! This seemed ironic as the few Westerners they encountered were probably backpackers whose grubby clothes were due to the filthy state of Chinese public transport!

Despite having window seats sleep proved elusive due to the discomfort, stifling heat and sheer volume of noise constantly generated by Chinese passengers. Arriving shattered into Beijing late morning, a taxi took us to Yong Ding Men Hotel. We checked in, filled out the usual excessive paperwork, paid up and crashed out for the rest of the day.

CHINA'S CAPITAL, FORMERLY known as Peking, is home to nine million people, and it looked like most of them rode bicycles. Riders swarmed everywhere, filling roads to capacity. Yong Ding sat in a side street and in an idle moment of curiosity, I counted the passing pedal traffic. During rush hour it would have been pointless to even try, but it was late afternoon with the traffic tide at a low ebb. In the space of sixty seconds, seventy bicycles passed by, but in rush hour, this would multiply tenfold. That meant that more than 100,000 cyclists would pedal past the hotel every day!

With bike rental now down to just ten pence a day, we kept them for the duration. Which was fine at the hotel but became a problem in a public bike park where thousands of identical models stood side by side. Only the bikes number and lock key set it apart, so it was crucial to remember its exact location. But this could prove a little tricky after a liquid lunch where the price of a pint of Beijing Beer equated to seven pence!

We strolled the massive expanse of Tiananmen Square where just three years earlier the military opened fire on crowds at a peaceful mass protest against corruption. Students and demonstrators calling for democratic reform occupied the square for seven weeks, but as the protest grew millions joined from around the country. At one point an estimated million protesters stood in Tiananmen Square. On 4th June 1989 tanks rumbled through the streets as the army moved in simultaneously from different directions, randomly firing at unarmed protesters. Hundreds, possibly even thousands, were killed during the government's shocking hard-line response.

Returning from the Russian embassy, we were stunned to see guards conducting their own pistol practice in the street. Only when a van rounded a corner and headed towards them were they forced to temporarily stop shooting!

ASIDE FROM MILLIONS of cyclists, the city is also home to hordes of idle folk who do little but squat in the street and watch the world go by. It's been endemic throughout China, but now in the capital, it's more like an epidemic.

Thousands more eke out livings by collecting cardboard or selling a few small fish or scrappy produce laid out on pavements. Others give haircuts on wooden stools out in the street or serve cha from little trolleys tucked against sidewalls.

Each morning opposite our hotel, endless queues of bicycle carts form waiting to load outside the Pepsi factory, but within minutes of pulling up, most riders are asleep on the rear platform. It seems much of the population spends half their time either asleep or squatting on haunches staring into space!

Further down the road old men clad in communist blue roll relaxation balls around their palms as they babysit caged birds dangling from clotheslines strung between trees. Sometimes they cycle with the cages swinging crazily from handlebars and the poor birds clinging desperately to their perches. Often the city air is so thick with pollution and eye-watering, throat-clogging dust that their precious pets would probably be better off indoors! With a major road and sewer system under construction, the dust and noise never stop. In six weeks we've seen little of the sun as the skies have been full of smog even away from the industrialised cities, despite the lack of motorised traffic.

BEIJING IS FULL of incredible sights and we explored the Forbidden City where a massive portrait of Chairman Mao guards the gateway. Inside its broad walls, a vast complex of 800 buildings was once the Imperial Palace homes to ruling Ming and Qing dynasties. For five hundred years the ancient royal city had been off-limits to civilians and the price of admission would have been instant death, but we ambled in for the cost of a few yuan.

Set amongst magnificent architecture is the grand staircase, a massive marble sculpture depicting nine dragons playing in clouds. Sandwiched between double staircases the three-metre-wide masterpiece stretches for over sixteen metres. Weighing 300 tonnes the immense intricately carved block is believed to have been dragged there 600 years ago using only ice and manpower. During winter, workers dug hundreds of wells along a 70 km route from the quarry, then poured water onto the road to form ice so the huge block could slide. Once in place inside the city walls, teams of sculptors began their skilful work.

The Forbidden City is the largest palace complex on the planet, covering 178 acres, and was constructed mainly from wood, which allowed it to move and survive the many earthquakes that have shaken Peking over the centuries.

TO ESCAPE CROWDS visiting the Great Wall we caught a bus to Mutianyu, climbed the steps and walked until we reached the unrestored part of the wall. Six of us sat on ancient stones of a watchtower gazing at the undulating path winding through the mountains, marvelling at its construction. Although overgrown with bushes and greenery, two lines of crumbling castellated stonework could still be seen snaking into the distance.

A massive slave labour force built the Mutianyu section of wall 1400 years ago. Aside from defining and defending a kingdom, it transported troops over the rugged terrain and was built broad enough to take horsemen riding five abreast. Steep mountainous terrain must have made construction almost impossible in parts, yet the Great Wall stretches for over five thousand miles.

WHEN I MET Casper back in Hong Kong, he'd already booked a seat aboard the Trans Mongolian train to Moscow, so he left Beijing a few days before me. I wanted to visit Fragrant Hills Park but couldn't persuade anyone else to make the long ride, so decided to cycle there solo.

I'd been cycling for well over an hour when I noticed a car creeping from a side street. As there was nothing to obscure the driver's view, I just moved out a little. But the closer I came the more he edged out, forcing me wider and wider. As I crossed in front of the bonnet, he drove into me sending me flying. My bike was bent, and I was bleeding, but the driver looked utterly unconcerned and had obviously done it on purpose. As I vented my anger, he stood with his two friends expressionlessly staring back at me.

With so many bikes in China, roadside repair shops are everywhere and I spotted one nearby. I made him push my bike over to the shack and pay for repairs. Then he drove away laughing with his friends! With cars being quite rare on the street, it was obvious he must have been wealthy and had probably knocked me off just for fun, or perhaps even for a bet!

My bike seemed ok so I carried on and at last, reached what I thought was the park, but after paying and going inside realised it was the Summer Palace! The vast Royal gardens cover over 700 acres and I'd visited before but must have come in a through a different gate. For Peking, it's an unusually peaceful place, so I decided to stay and forget Fragrant Hills Park as that was further still to cycle.

Kunming Lake takes up three-quarters of the park and was expanded and hand-dug deeper by an emperor with the help of 100,000 labourers! Its cool waters are surrounded by forested hills dotted with thousands of ancient structures, pavilions and ornate temples. Sculpted multi-arched bridges rise above floating carpets of lily pads, and a large boat made from marble lives permanently by the lakeshore. The park also homes the Long Corridor, a 700m covered walkway richly decorated with 14,000 paintings depicting scenes from Chinese mythology.

With black clouds fast approaching, I set off back to the city but missed a turn in a huge dust storm whipped up by wind and soon got lost. With daylight fading, I gambled on a dirt track heading in the right direction and felt very alone as I rode past a shanty town of cardboard homes alongside a river. My gamble paid off and with great relief, got my bearings again in the sprawling megacity. Two and a half hours later I finally made it back to the hostel, bloodied, bruised and blackened from head to toe in plastered on grime. It had been an eventful day but at least I didn't lose my bike deposit as the damage went unnoticed!

As I awaited departure aboard the Trans Mongolian train, it felt like I was killing time for my last few days in Beijing. With an onward flight booked from Moscow I was less than two weeks from home, and after almost two years on the road was itching to see my family.

And after the bike incident, I couldn't wait to leave China and its billion staring faces behind!

Trans Mongolian Express: Six days on a train

Day 1: Bai Bai China

OUR LAST CHANCE to stock up with booze would be at the Chinese border, warned Monkey Business's scrappy photocopied brochure. It also noted that Chinese alcohol should be labelled as aftershave and the only reason to buy it would be to give to a Russian you disliked!

With five days ahead of us on the train, we shared the same thought that we weren't prepared to risk running out of alcohol, even if it did taste a little like aftershave! In fact, everyone aboard seemed to have the same idea, resulting in a chaotic scene as a crush of frantic passengers waved fistfuls of cash towards two nonplussed Chinese staff. Soon the rowdy crowd had cleared the shelves of booze, and Russians bought everything else for sale in the station's small shop.

Our train disappeared to have bogies changed due to the different track gauge in Mongolia, so with time to kill we held an impromptu leaving party. It was cold on the concrete platform so we moved our little celebration inside the Bank of China where we'd spotted empty seats.

Everybody seemed happy to be leaving China behind

and as we sat guzzling Beijing Beer, many stories of hard travelling got shared. I'd been in the country for seven weeks and it had been an amazing experience, but everything had been such hard work and so full of frustration it had taken the edge off from the adventure.

Language had, of course, been a major barrier, along with the signs written in hanzi, making something as simple as taking a train a real challenge. Then there were the vast distances involved and the discomfort, filth and constant din of travelling through China by bus or by train.

Currency hadn't helped much either with FEC's, yuan, fen, jao, mao and kuai to contend with. Having to pay highly inflated tourist prices and then having to use more valuable FEC's for the privilege had been especially galling. Even though China was cheap, every yuan counts when you're on an extended trip, and I was now accumulating debt on a credit card!

The daily frustrations of trying to do basic things and getting around seem to have worn everyone down, along with unfriendly, unhelpful attitudes of the Chinese. I'd grown accustomed to the constant dead-eyed deadpan stares, but the rudeness of people has been harder to accept. Countless times on the street my guidebook has been grabbed by a nosy passerby. In a market, I had my arm and chest hair examined and tugged by two laughing locals, who then fetched their giggling girlfriends. We went through the routine again until I said "Do you want a look down here too?" and made to undo my jeans. At which point it had the desired effect, and they quickly departed! The novelty of body hair must have been new to them, but their utter disregard for me was incredulous. I'd started to understand how circus freaks must have felt.

Along with many amazing sights my trip has been marked with a host of unpleasant ones, from the live skinned rabbit in Canton and the horse being chopped up roadside, to a newborn baby lying discarded amongst a pile of litter.

China has a one-child policy, and I'd been told me it wasn't uncommon for poor mothers to be forced to abandon babies. A family could have to pay up to 2000 yuan to keep a second child when the average monthly wage was only around 250. But even so, to have left the baby in such an uncaring way was beyond belief.

Throughout China, the near-constant daily soundtrack has been the horrible sound of hawking, the prelude to somebody spitting on the floor. It made no difference where they were, be it in the street, on a busy bus or train, even inside a restaurant. The disgusting habit is common through all age groups irrespective of gender. Here at the border, there is even a prominent red and white pictorial sign on the wall to discourage the national pastime of spitting!

So, as we sat awaiting our modified train, the consensus was despite the fascination with China and its incredible sights, everybody was pleased to be leaving the country behind.

ABOARD THE CARRIAGE, our passports came back with exit stamps and we shunted across no-man's-land to the Mongolian border. We waited in line, filled in yet more forms, and handed the passports over to a fearsome looking female official straight out of a sixties spy film!

By the time we climbed into bunks, it was the early hours of the morning, but just two hours later I got awoken again by a heavy fist pounding on the door when they decided to return our documents.

FIVE MINUTES LATER than its scheduled departure time the Trans Mongolian Express had pulled away from Beijing's main station at 7.40 the previous morning. But with six days ahead of us aboard the train, time was soon to become insignificant!

After enduring too many grim trains through China, the compartment surprised me as it had a carpet, curtains and for the first time looked clean. Sharing the cosy space of four bunks and a small table were Eugenine from Holland and Heidi and Burckhardt from Germany.

The first day slipped by fast as we swapped stories and got to know each other, but outside the dull scenery remained unchanged. The train crossed endless barren plains backdropped by undulating hills on the horizon. Remote, insignificant settlements would occasionally interrupt the monotonous landscape where a few hardy souls could be seen scratching a living off the land. Other than a few horses and flocks of sheep we saw little else.

Travel dominated the conversation, along with much

complaining about the food in the dining car, its extortionate prices and the usual frosty-faced unhelpful Chinese staff, who didn't know the meaning of service. But once we reached the border the restaurant car would be changed to a Mongolian one.

So as we sat celebrating inside the Bank of China that was one more reason to be pleased to be leaving the country behind!

MOONSKY STAR, A.K.A. Monkey Business, who I'd organised my ticket and visa through back in Hong Kong, advised bringing biscuits to bribe our carriage conductor would ensure being well looked after. But with rumours of short food supplies on board, everybody seemed reluctant to hand over anything at all. I had a few packs of instant noodles, but after the first forkful regretted buying them, so wouldn't be passing any precious biscuits to the attendant. The noodles tasted no worse than the dining car's offerings but at least I didn't have to go through sixty doors just to get to them!

Day 2: Into Mongolia

I AWOKE TO dazzling sunlight glaring off an endless expanse of undulating sand. Outside my window, the fine particles got whipped into a swirling frenzy by the pace of our passing train, and the vast ocean of sand stretched to the horizon without interruption.

After the broken night's sleep, I took a while to rouse myself from the top bunk, by which time the rippled sands of the Gobi desert had started to sprout clumps of hardy grasses. As the train rattled onwards, these patches grew into vast open plains of rolling grassland sliced in two by steel rail tracks running unwaveringly west.

Now and again, in the middle of nowhere, a tiny community of attractive buildings would be passed but there seemed no apparent reason for their existence. It was almost as if they had been dropped from space and had settled where they landed.

Later, these sturdy looking houses were replaced by yurts which appeared equally incongruous and lost amidst the immense open landscape. With white sides and low-pitched roofs, the circular traditional tents of nomadic herders looked too futuristic dotted on the infinite grasslands. In complete contrast to their natural surroundings, they resembled something from an early sci-fi movie and might have looked less out of place on the moon.

Yesterday we only made a few brief stops, and today has been the same. The first came at Choyr, where there was little to see but it felt great to just be off the train, breathe fresh air and walk on something stationary. Later, came a second much longer stop at Ulaanbaatar, Mongolia's capital.

In contrast to the drab tower blocks and dull sixties architecture, the Mongolian people looked bright and sharp, although it's possible this was because many were trying illicitly to sell us stuff and had to watch out for police! On the spartan paved platform Mongols dressed in Western-style clothes mingled with horsemen clad in long leather boots and flowing great-coats wrapped with red cummerbunds.

Our expensive transit visas for Mongolia forbade us to stray beyond the platform, but the temptation to explore further proved too strong to resist. But as we never knew how long the train would stop for, it was too risky to venture far.

I bought a brick-like loaf of bread from a furtive kid darting around the platform, thinking it would make a change from noodles as meals in the Mongolian dining car had turned out to be disappointing. Again the prices are way over-inflated and the staff more interested in selling gloves and other goods on the side, than serving any food!

DESPITE MONGOLIA'S LARGE land mass, its population is only around two million, but the inhospitable Gobi desert to the south covers a third of the country and is still growing. Now, a peaceful nation of nomadic herders, eight hundred years ago things were very different for Mongols when Genghis Khan ruled. His armies of ruthless warriors conquered huge chunks of Asia and China, creating the largest land empire in history. According to legend when Genghis was buried in 1227 his funeral escort slayed everyone they encountered to keep the gravesite secret and then diverted a river course over it so it could never be found!

THE EMPTY LANDSCAPE remained that way all day apart

from the odd yurt, occasional herds of horses, sheep or small groups of camels. I spotted a solitary eagle soaring high above on thermals, and infrequent flocks of scrawny rooks scrounging meagre livings.

During the night we reached the border with the Soviet Union where a guard roused me from a drunken slumber to fill in yet more forms and hand over my passport again. Earlier, an American celebrated her birthday in the dining car and, despite its dubious flavour, Chinese champagne had been flowing. After that, I needed several beers to take away the taste and unwisely washed those down with shots of deadly Chinese vodka.

Around dawn, I half awoke to the troubling thought that the train was moving but I hadn't got my passport back, then, deciding it was now too late to do anything about it went straight back to sleep! When at last I surfaced, I felt relieved to see it lying safely on the table.

Day 3: Inside the Soviet Union

IT WAS A quiet day in the carriage with everyone nursing hangovers, also it was an extra long one as we changed over to Moscow time. This meant putting the clocks back a full five hours but actually made little difference as time has become meaningless after two whole days aboard the train.

We now have a Russian restaurant car and like the previous ones, it has different opening times. We have never known whether the car was using Beijing time,

Mongolian time, local time or Moscow time. Our carriage is at the opposite end to the dining car, and every carriage in between is an obstacle course of bulky cardboard boxes blocking the aisle. Squeezing and sloaming along these passageways packed with goods and people took time as did navigating all the doors on the moving train. Sometimes we made the slow journey only to find the restaurant closed and had to turn around and work our way back again. Each round trip involved 120 doors, so was really frustrating when it proved fruitless!

COMING FROM MONGOLIA into Siberia the contrast has been stark. Gone are the open expanses of endless grassland, instead, the scenery has changed to a captivating untamed wilderness of forests, low hills and clear rivers. The sporadic towns we passed boasted attractive tin-roofed wooden buildings with brightly painted shutters, but as the day progressed and we rattled relentlessly west, the towns became more run down. An impression exacerbated by the miserable weather.

Siberia covers an area of over five million miles, making it bigger than Canada, the second largest country and the region equates to almost 10% of Earth's land mass. Later, the tracks would lead us to the shores of Lake Baikal, the world's oldest and deepest lake, which holds 20% of the planets non-frozen freshwater and plunges to depths of a mile!

BY MID-AFTERNOON, THE combination of hangovers and

the monotony of slow passing hours conspired to dull the mood inside our carriage, until we made a stop in Ulan Ude. As we eased to a halt, crowds of waiting Russians mobbed the carriages. Windows down the length of the train had sprouted price boards and frantic trading was in progress. Bundles of roubles and handfuls of hard currency were passed across in exchange for dresses, shoes, leather jackets and Adidas t-shirts.

People were climbing up and clinging onto windows to bargain with Chinese traders and pass goods down to the money-waving hordes below. It was a crazy scene as locals frantically fought to buy goods, and with the train only ever officially stopping for fifteen minutes at most, became a race against time.

Throughout the afternoon and into the night this frenetic scene got repeated at every station, and we realised we were riding a moving marketplace. With three Trans Siberian trains coming through each week this has become the main supply line direct from Beijing.

WE MADE THE slow trek to the new Russian restaurant car, without high hopes for any improvement in the dining experience, and as we entered our fears appeared confirmed. The dishevelled waiter looked like a down-and-out alcoholic, and the huge female chef resembled a mud wrestler, but appearances can be deceptive and they were not only helpful but efficient. After seven weeks of Chinese so-called service, this came as a nice surprise and better still, the food turned out to be excellent. We dined like kings on caviar and drank champagne to celebrate, and with the main course, my bill came to less than two bucks!

Day 4: Half distance, but now becoming dangerous

LAST NIGHT TURNED into an eventful one when a window got smashed just a few compartments along. Eva and Gerda were sitting with Inga and a few others when an iron bar was hurled at the window. The bar bounced off, so the Soviet on the platform picked it up and threw it again, and this time the window smashed showering glass inside. The assailant reached up and grabbed the first thing he felt, which fortunately happened to only be a bottle of beer, and he ran off with that. It was lucky nobody got injured but was a close call and a scare for the girls. In another incident, a Chinese trader ended up with a black eye after being punched by an angry Russian who thought he'd been cheated.

Our door is now being regularly pulled open by Russians scoping out the compartment. It's obvious what they are doing but they don't blink an eye at our blunt words and gestures. Even with one of us standing in the doorway, they will still poke their heads past and have a good look at what we've got inside.

The problem is the train is full of traders with goods and money, and our carriage is full of Westerners with backpacks, cameras and cash, and it's become clear that locals are bribing their way aboard looking for opportunities to steal.

The door opening started as an annoyance, but as the day has progressed, it's increased to a worrying degree. Ever more Russians are climbing on board, and we have near-constant interruptions from them. It's reached the point where we can't risk leaving our compartment empty and now go in pairs to the dining car. Before, we just locked it and left.

Burckhardt complained to our carriage attendant, who seemed reluctant to help, so after losing patience, he confronted two guys loitering outside, but was threatened with a flick knife and forced to back off.

Earlier a Walkman was stolen when a brazen thief climbed the side of the train and reached in through a top window. At every station, the frantic trading has become more and more out of control and it's felt like it wouldn't take much to erupt into a riot. The desperate scenes we are witnessing could be a direct result of the collapse of the Soviet Union, which happened only last year.

We no longer feel safe to explore at stops, instead, the group stays gathered just outside our carriage. Several times travellers have been told menacingly to stop taking photos as they tried to record what is happening here.

The whole mood aboard the carriage has now changed, and we are no longer being offered anything for sale at stations. Instead, for the locals its buy, buy, buy. Or steal, steal, steal.

Apart from the trouble, the day has been a strange

one, due partly to the time change and everyone is wandering around in a daze yawning and wondering what's going on. Yesterday we still had 5000 more kilometres to reach Moscow, but today we passed the halfway marker at 3932 km. It's staggering to think after travelling for three and a half days that we have only made it halfway! But with the border crossings and their associated delays behind us, the second half should be quicker.

Day 5: The Army Arrives

TODAY IT SEEMS our driver is at last, putting his foot down and we are now a mere 2200 km from Mockba. Yesterday we were still five hours behind schedule due to holdups at the borders. According to Heidi's book, the Trans-Mongolian train averages 69 kph over the six days, and with the help of trackside distance from Moscow markers, we have calculated the driver is doing 100 kph. It feels the fastest stretch so far, but last night's ride felt too fast as it was a real rib-rattler spent rolling across the bunk and banging into the steel sidebars.

This morning Eva left her compartment whilst the others still slept, and in her short absence someone reached in and grabbed the nearest bag. Fortunately, only her wash bag had been stolen.

All the officials seem to be corrupt, from the customs to the conductors, and perhaps even the police. Carrying long leather truncheons, police are now patrolling the train, but even they seem to scope the compartments out.

Last night on a platform I passed two in a huddle with locals, and as I walked by something got hidden away from my view. I ambled on further and glanced back. It was a gun.

There is little doubt the conductors are accepting bribes from Russians who climb aboard and steal their way through the train before getting off at the next stop. Some even have copies of the compartment keys. At one border crossing, customs officials told four Chinese traders to leave their compartment so it could be searched. On return, they discovered a bag missing, so beat the official until he handed the bag back!

It's the traders who are the main problem because if they weren't on board then the train would be much less of a target. But with so much money to be made I'm sure it will continue. A Russian passenger told me he could make $3000 in a single trip, buying stock in Beijing and selling his way home.

TODAY'S STOPS HAVE felt a little safer than yesterday, and there now seems less activity at our door. Also, we've been offered goods to buy again at stations, which we hope is a good sign. I was shown a watch for five bucks and Inge got a bottle of champagne for 200 roubles, equating to about a dollar. Much better value than a bottle of vodka bought earlier, which turned out to be water!

LATE AFTERNOON WE pulled alongside a platform and as usual, a large crowd was waiting, but also assembled were a squad of armed soldiers who stopped the mob from approaching. One guy who reached the train got grabbed by the throat and dragged away. It looked an overreaction to what he'd done, but the military here are not messing about.

Despite earlier signs, the mood once again changed when a French traveller discovered someone had stolen his backpack whilst he slept. He'd lost almost everything he had. Everyone felt outraged, and we agreed to search the train, but the attendant was no help at all and forbade it.

These officials are also at the root of the problem as it's them who allow outsiders onto the train. They get paid to do a job, take bribes to top up their wages and then ignore their duties. Even the patrolling police have said they are helpless to control the fast degenerating situation. There are now three smashed windows I know of, and I'm wondering what the hell will happen next.

WE DISCOVERED THE dining car will be closed tomorrow as they have almost run out of supplies. With the prospect of no more food, we spent our time filling up with anything they had left, and realising there would be no alcohol either, took the last opportunity to top those levels up too. Resulting in a tricky slow stagger back to our carriage, through the corridor obstacle course which was now even more challenging!

Day 6: Arrival in Mockba

SO TODAY IS our last day aboard the Trans-Mongolian Market Express and we are now back in Europe having passed a marker yesterday showing we had left Asia. This morning we have a mere 700 km to go to reach the last stop on the line; Moscow. The train is still running five hours behind so arrival will be late afternoon instead of around midday.

Life in compartment three has settled into not quite a routine, but perhaps just more of an acceptance of our temporary home and it's strange to think soon we will get off for good.

ALTHOUGH THE END was in sight, the day seemed the slowest of the trip which wasn't helped by the fact the dining car had closed. As we impatiently watched the countdown markers numbers get lower, it became a day of scrounging for leftovers. But pickings were slim, and we shared biscuits and bland noodles with the odd, strange Chinese sweet discovered in the depths of a backpack.

At one station the lack of food almost cost four of us our seats for the final stretch. The guidebook mentioned that at certain stops it should be possible to buy potatoes with chives from old ladies on the platform. With hopes of tasty hot snacks, we leapt off and went searching for old crones selling spuds. A kiosk was spotted, so we ran across the tracks, but as we reached it another train pulled in hiding ours from view. The long train took forever to come to a standstill and to our horror when it finally stopped we could see ours moving off and hear our friends shouting at us. I ducked straight under the nearest carriage and ran full pelt, but everyone was still yelling and I realised Gerda was oblivious to the cries. I leapt aboard and joined the frantic shouting. With a pounding heart, I watched two others run and jump aboard before Gerda finally made it. In her panic, she tripped and fell sprawling face-down on the tracks, before picking herself up and sprinting towards us.

The spuds were tasty, but the incident was way too close for comfort. We'd been warned to never leave the train without passports but hadn't always stuck to that in our haste to get off at unannounced brief stops. The consequences of being left behind with your luggage, friends and passport still on the train, didn't bear thinking about.

AT FIVE-THIRTY WE arrived at our destination. We'd been aboard the train for one hundred and thirty-five hours and had covered 7865 kilometres.

As I stepped off the Trans Mongolian Express for the final time I looked up to see the huge Mockba sign towering over the station, along with a giant Soviet hammer and sickle.

Moscow. At last!

South America
1997

Trekking in Iceberg Territory

THE CAT FROZE. Flattening itself into the road, it stared wide-eyed in alarm at my approach. It was three a.m, and I was weaving unsteadily home from a party. I stopped, swayed a little and then blinked slowly at the cat to show I posed no threat. It seemed reassured. Slightly.

It was then I noticed a single Monopoly Chance card lying on the path, and bent to pick it up. I turned it over.

Advance To Go!

Surely that must be a sign.

I looked around for more cards but only saw the cat. Now having a wash…

Two days earlier I'd been sitting at work staring out of an office window at PFL, bored and searching for inspiration. I'd been back in the UK for five years, following my twenty-two-month adventure through Australasia. I wanted to rediscover that freedom, to explore and live the dream again. But this time it would need to be somewhere more challenging.

South America! Distant, and possibly dangerous.

Perfect. Decision made!

Back at work on Monday, I handed my notice in, having booked a one-way flight to Santiago de Chile. My plan was simple, land and head north. That was it. No research, no schedule and no return ticket. Real adventure. Proper travel!

The decision was taken and acted upon so quickly I soon discovered there wasn't enough time to complete my course of jabs, leaving me little option but carry the last rabies dose, in its tiny glass phial, along with me on the plane.

Fate was kind as I was seated beside a friendly English speaking Swiss-Chilean being met by her son, and upon landing, between them persuaded a reluctant airport medic to administer my vital jab. The son then drove me closer to the city, dropping me off at a bus stop.

A friend had recommended a safe place to stay, and I soon found the dilapidated building ironically named Hotel Nuevo. I had little command of Spanish so the receptionist showed me to a room and used his finger to write the price in dust on its cracked mirror!

Ugly brown and mustard artex adorned its walls, and over the years floor tiles had been randomly replaced, resulting in a chaotic mishmash of styles and colour. A stained, lumpy mattress lay atop a bed curved like a banana, only one tap worked and the door wouldn't close! But the old place was cheap and full of fellow backpackers.

This turned out to be the first of three stays in the Nuevo, and each time my room had even more character. One had a toilet attached by a single loose nail which tipped over if I sat too fast after dining on dodgy street food. Another had a two-foot-long hole in its floor. Large enough to watch street life four stories below!

Chatting with other travellers in the Nuevo I heard tales about Torres del Paine in Patagonia and decided I wanted to see it for myself. So after just three days in the country, my plan changed. I headed south!

With no return ticket, and no schedule to follow I had the luxury of time, giving me freedom to go with the flow and make it up as I went along. One of the many pleasures of long-term travel.

TORRES DEL PAINE National Park is located on the southern tip of Chile, way down in Patagonia, making it amongst the world's most remote parks. The country's capital, Santiago de Chile, lies 2000 km to the north. That's by air, but by road, it's closer to three thousand. Puerto Natales is the closest town to the park but even that is 150 km away, or around three hours by bus.

Covering an area of 1600 square kilometres, the park is home to more than 100 species of birds, two dozen types of mammals and over 200 species of plants. Its scenery is spectacular with stunning landscapes at every turn. Everything within this rugged park is on a grand scale with towering snow-capped peaks, mighty glaciers and vast lakes dotted with immense icebergs. Because of its remote location, the park doesn't see many visitors and remains unspoilt and untouched. Official figures recorded only 38,000 visitors a few years earlier, so you could hike for hours or maybe even days without seeing another soul.

THE SOUND WAS loud and terrifying. And close. It woke me in an instant.

Lying alone in a tiny tent, pitched on the edge of a precipice, to one side a barrier of branches, to the other a few metres of uneven rock. Then a sheer drop to a glacier. Two hundred feet below.

FUCK! AVALANCHE!

I'd seen snow high above me during the past three days, and beyond my barrier, a steep slope rose through trees to an unseen height above me…

ARRIVING JUST BEFORE dusk, I'd hoped to reach the official site at Campo Paso, but had no way of knowing how much further it was or how treacherous the trail would be. So I had no choice but to pitch an illegal camp for the night. Having hiked for eight hours I felt tired and knew it would be foolhardy to push on as the terrain had been getting more extreme all day.

I'd been searching for a water source and found a small stream just as daylight was fading. It was sluggish which wasn't ideal but I filled my water bottles and backtracked to the cliff edge above Grey Glacier.

It was a spectacular and awe-inspiring place to camp but I had no time to admire the view. I got water heating on the stove and set about clearing a spot for my tent. Boulders and tree stumps covered the unforgiving ground, but using a large rock I scraped, smashed and dug until I scoured a space big enough. Despite my hard work, the lumpy ground was far from level, but it would have to do and I prayed the groundsheet wouldn't get pierced as I pitched my tent in the half-light.

THROUGHOUT THE DAY, I'd endured gale force winds so severe that gusts sometimes stopped me mid-stride. To make headway, I had to walk leaning so far forward that if the wind had lulled, I would have fallen over. Having experienced the immense power of Patagonian wind I knew my pitch was precarious and vulnerable, so with this in mind, secured the tent with as much weight as possible. I piled branch after heavy branch on top of one another until a three-foot wall of dead wood curved around its windward side.

With the tent as protected as much as possible, I devoured my pasta in gloom as I gazed out across the lighter expanse of the glacier. Soon it was pitch black, and I slid into my sleeping bag hoping for a long night's rest.

The days hiking had been incredible with more jaw-dropping scenery and miles of tough challenging trails. Leaving Pehoe lake shore camp behind in light rain an easy route led up the valley to another vast windswept lake, which I flanked along a rocky trail. All morning I battled a howling headwind before getting temporary respite as the track dipped into trees. Two hours into the hike I crested a rise and the magnificent sight of Grey Glacier stopped me in my tracks. Gazing down the length of wind-ravaged Lago Grey, icebergs the size of stadiums dotted the lake and led my eye towards the face of the spectacular glacier. Even from several miles away its scale was incredible.

Rising seventy feet above frigid waters and measuring four kilometres across with a massive rocky island splitting the middle, the glacier stretched to the horizon sandwiched between snow-capped crags. With not a soul in sight or any sign of human activity, it was a stunning scene.

For the next hour, the track clung to mountainside and so did I in some ferocious gusts. When sunlight broke through, the huge icebergs revealed incredible sculpting and intense shades of icy-blue, and the illuminated glacier looked even more breathtaking.

Reaching the campsite at Refugio Grey I stopped to make lunch, then walked to a lookout facing the glacier, arriving moments too late to witness a calving. I heard a loud crashing roar and raced ahead in time to see a tidal wave surging away from the face, the result of a huge ice collapse.

After camp, the terrain became ever more challenging, and I crossed ravines carved by cascading torrents and scrambled on all fours up treacherous unstable slopes. Amongst the trees, massive fallen trunks blocked the trail which had to be straddled with care, whilst steep muddy banks left no alternative but slide down with little control. The toughest stretch was a near vertical descent through mud and running water with no footholds. Entrusting my safety to a length of old rope tied to a loose wooden stake, I tackled it backwards hoping nothing would break.

By the time I found the camp spot it had been a long, physical day, so I crawled straight into my sleeping bag after wolfing down the pasta. But sleep came far too slowly, due in part to the angle of the pitch, which was still too steep despite my digging. Rocks poked through my thin roll mat, making comfort elusive, but mainly it was the biting cold, despite being cocooned by a thickly quilted bag. Soon I was wearing all my clothes but still felt too cold to sleep. At some point I dozed out of sheer exhaustion, dreaming of puma, which wandered these trials along with the occasional tourist…

AND THEN I heard it. An immense powerful roaring sound. A sound that filled me with instant terror. A sound that was getting rapidly closer.

I was wide awake in a second as the thought of being swept off the mountainside shot through my mind. Moments later the tent was flattened by a massive force of wind slamming into it.

At once relieved it wasn't an avalanche I now faced the real possibility of wind ripping my tent off the slope and tossing it over the precipice. There were still many hours of darkness before daybreak, so I couldn't abandon the shelter as there was nowhere to go. With no other options, all I could do was lay protected inside the tent and pray my weight would keep it in place.

The wind strength was so severe I doubted the tent

would survive the night, so crammed everything into my backpack in preparation for an emergency evacuation.

The constant threat of being torn off the mountain-side kept me on full alert ready to scramble out, if I got the chance, as wind continued to scream at incredible volume through the trees. All night I lay balled up and freezing whilst the wind relentlessly battered my flimsy tent. It was fortunate I'd found so many weighty boughs for my barrier as without them the tent would have been blown away, with me still inside.

By early dawn, the winds had eased a little and as soon as I could see vague shapes I crawled out and lit the stove, relieved to have made it through the night.

SUNRISE REVEALED A spectacular view. Beneath me, the massive glacier stretched into the distance. Dazzling snow, streaked with hundreds of blue crevasses ran across the five-kilometre wide tongue. Beyond, a range of rugged snow-capped mountains backdropped the frozen expanse. To the south, the immense glacier dipped then plunged into Lago Grey's iceberg-strewn waters.

Whilst my porridge bubbled, I broke camp and rolled up the tent, randomly redistributing branches around. Minutes after scraping the last lumps from my pan a Conaf park ranger showed up on horseback and silently surveyed the scene. One sleepy gringo with backpack, one tent shaped space in the ground and one heck of a view. Camping outside a handful of dedicated sites is prohibited within the park, but he just fixed me with a stern glare, before nodding and ambling away.

It was going to be another great day; I had survived the storm, hadn't been mauled by pumas and now even the ranger had chosen to ignore my activities!

I WAS NOW halfway through my rations, so couldn't venture any deeper into the park, but instead had the pleasure of backtracking to Camp Pehoe, with the bonus of a slightly lighter pack. Lugging a large SLR camera, camping kit and supplies for six days was hard work, so every meal reduced my load. In a desperate effort to cut down weight in my backpack I'd eaten all the tinned food on day one, which meant a boring menu from then on. Two camps had small shops but there were no guarantees provisions would be available in the park, so all food had to be carried. Also, although water was safe to drink from streams and rivers, I never knew when the next refill would come, so had to lug the weight of that along too.

Heading back I caught up with Ami, an Israeli I knew from a hostel, so we hiked together to the refugio, making a risky off-piste excursion right down to the glacier face en route. Dwarfed by the towering frozen structure, I lingered only long enough for photos and scrambled away fearful of an ice collapse, as we'd heard several already.

Resting at the refugio I dozed off in the sun, which then didn't leave much time to return to Pehoe. So I donned my mochila once more and made a two-and-a-half hour forced march to reach camp before nightfall.

Arriving shattered, I found the camp by the lakeshore again being pounded by brutal winds. I squeezed my tent into a tiny space between the protection of some bushes, cooked yet more pasta, tossed the empty pans outside and fell into a long deep sleep.

OVER MORE BREAKFAST porridge I decided Pehoe would make a perfect base camp, so I tipped out my pack, pushed in some food and layers and set off for the French Glacier.

Walking with a near empty pack was a joy as I followed an easy, pleasant trail along the turquoise lake. But the sight of what I presumed to be the hanging French Glacier was disappointing, and the trail didn't even go near it. Deciding to get a closer look I started scrambling over rocks and forcing a way up through coarse, steep terrain. After thirty minutes I could go no further, so descended at a tangent hoping to pick up the trail. When I found it I bumped into Tim, an American I'd met on day one, who told me he'd just got back from the French Glacier, which was still miles away! So my tough unnecessary detour had cost me an hour, wasted energy, and a beer. But I wasn't to discover that until much later...

Bidding farewell to Tim I trekked onwards, risking ageing suspension bridges strung above churning white-water and traversing steep trails over mountainside crisscrossed by waterfalls. Later, the track plunged into dark forests or wound across exposed plains where I battled the ever-present wind. Sun-bleached, wind-sculpted trees stood where they'd succumbed to gales, surrounded by giant snapped boughs. Finally, I got to the impressive French Glacier and continued my climb up to Campo Britanico.

By the time I reached the top, it was late afternoon, the weather was closing in and my boots were sodden from squelching through a wide bog. Forcing down the last of my rock-hard, five-day-old bread rolls, I took a few photos and started back for base.

It was New Year's Eve, so I wanted to get back to the camp shop to buy some celebratory beer before it closed, which meant doing the four-and-a-half hour hike in well under three. It was a tall order, but I had to try…

MY LIGHT PACK and the downhill slope helped, as the thought of my first beer in a week drove me forwards. At Campo Italiano I stopped briefly to warm by a campfire when I spotted Ami again. With the smell of food cooking on the fire, it was tempting to stay longer, but I wanted my tent and a cool beer.

By the time I reached Pehoe lakeshore, I felt exhausted but pushed on as fast as I could, knowing the camp was getting close. At last, I reached the shop but found its door locked. No beer for me tonight. I'd missed it closing by less than fifteen minutes as it turned out my watch was slow. Dejected, I wove my way wearily back to my tent and collapsed inside. All that effort only to miss out by minutes. Oh well, at least I had more packet soup and pasta left!!

AGAIN THE WIND howled incessantly all night and once more my tent survived the onslaught intact. But lying awake pre-dawn listening to the ferocious gale I doubted the ferry would run in the morning. My plan had been to have an easy final day, first taking the ferry across the lake, and then with luck, hitching a lift to Park Admin office to hook up with the afternoon bus heading back to Puerto Natales.

So after a wake-up coffee I rolled out of the tent and tried to walk, but after five days of hiking my feet were covered in blisters, and my calves were killing me as I hobbled towards the camp shop.

Once again I found it closed but now saw a sign saying no ferries were running as it was New Year's Day. Blinded by disappointment last night, somehow I'd failed to see the large notice.

This left me with a problem as I needed to leave today. I'd planned to explore the park for five days, but this was my sixth and I hadn't enough provisions for breakfast let alone another day. My only option was to hike out the long way round; a five-hour walk and not an appealing prospect. The bus would depart from the park office at two, and I had to catch it as there would be no other buses today.

I cooked all the provisions I had left; spaghetti mixed with powdered mash, flavoured by packet gravy!

Finishing that delicacy I broke camp and set off slowly. Every footstep felt painful, and I didn't want to continue for five minutes let alone five hours. But there was no alternative, so I forced myself onwards one step after another.

The track leading from camp climbed steadily making it tough right from the start, but later levelled and I walked along a wide grassy plain with the wind, for once, behind me. The implications of missing the bus drove me forwards and once I got into a rhythm, found I could zone out most of the pain. By the time I came to the first camp I was slightly ahead of schedule, so stopped to make coffee. It was a relief to sit and rest but made setting off again hard.

After several more hours, with the help of strong tailwinds, I reached Park Administration Office and collapsed with relief to await the bus.

By late afternoon I was back in Puerto Natales and soon working my way through a huge plate of food, this time without pasta or gravy!

Two days later I was comfortably bunked in Backpackers Paradise in Punta Arenas for cards, beer and a lazy recovery. The violent winds had still not abated and our small hostel was rocked by recorded gusts of 160 km per hour.

Several travellers were waiting to hitch a lift with a Naval expedition to Antarctica and I joined them on daily visits to watch the boat being prepped for the voyage. My budget wouldn't stretch to that adventure, so instead I was soon back aboard a coach, Santiago bound once more.

It seemed we had only just started the long haul north when our driver slowed to an early stop, executed a tricky ten point turn on the narrow tarmac and headed back from where we had come.

Fifteen minutes later I was still wondering what the hell he could have forgotten when we reached the main junction. This time, our driver turned left, onto the road heading north. The road he should have taken the first time!

So, less than an hour into the trip, the driver had already made a wrong turn when there were only two roads to choose between.

Quite worrying as this leg of the journey was likely to be at least thirty-six hours!

Chilean Recipe

TAKE THE COMPLETE Cheddar Gorge in one whole chunk and cleave to four times its depth, then widen fivefold. Spread evenly and thickly for two hundred kilometres. Next, pour in copious quantities of water, mixing wild torrents of aquamarine glacial water with calm crystal-clear backwaters, foaming waterfalls and huge fjords of saltwater.

For colour add vast swathes of lilac and white lupins. Decorate profusely with greenery, from open flat pastures to dense rainforests. Into the pastures toss giant trees, twist grotesquely, then bleach with sunlight. Snap lots of these brutally in half and stir in hundreds more felled specimens. Leave to rot where they land.

Sprinkle in a pinch of population and scatter randomly in tiny hamlets or tumbledown woodman's huts. Wind in a single tortuous dirt track snaking beneath snow-capped mist enshrouded crags, then for a more adventurous flavour chuck in challenging detours around landslides and washed out bridges.

Now enjoy, for eight hours…

THIS WAS WRITTEN following a minibus marathon from Coyhaique to Puyuhuapi with three fellow backpackers and a few locals. The fare for the spectacular trip may have been only a few dollars, but the cost to my sanity and hearing was considerably higher. Our driver owned just one tape, which he played non-stop at full volume for the duration. Chilean accordion music must be an acquired taste. And one I did not want!

My eyeballs were so constantly rattled by the corrugated road that Sellotape would have been useful to keep them still. It may have helped our driver too, as we had several near collisions on the narrow track and one, fortunately minor, head-on with another minibus!

WEEKS EARLIER WHILST staying at the Nuevo in Santiago I met a friendly Scottish couple curiously called The Beepers and then bumped into them again at a backpacker's in Pucon. We were all heading south, so decided to travel together along with Julia, another friend from the hostel.

Nobody was keen to take the normal gringo trail route to Patagonia, which entailed four slow days aboard the infamous Navimag ferry. Instead, we planned to start our journey on Chiloe Island. But according to the backpacker's bible (South American Handbook), it sounded challenging to link a route overland beyond the small island.

Chiloe is home to just 116,000 people, spread in a handful of settlements over the islands 250 km length. Known for its scenic beauty and traditional handicrafts as well as hundreds of all-wooden churches which dot the landscape, dating back to the eighteenth century. Having evolved in relative isolation from the mainlands influences Chiloe has a unique style of architecture including lots of stilt houses called palafitos. Many islanders, or Chilotes, are involved in the fishing industry or harvest the prolific seaweed to supply the Japanese market.

Mythology and superstition are strong amongst the island folk and strange stories abound involving ghost ships, witches, warlocks and even forest dwelling trolls!

REACHING CHILOE FROM Pucon meant a long day spent on too many buses, first to Valdivia, then Osorno, followed by Puerto Montt and Pargua. A ferry took us to Chacoa on the north of the island, then yet another bus on to Ancud. Our final leg was a hot, pack-laden, uphill slog in search of accommodation. With that sorted it was straight down to the harbour to watch the sun slip away over plates of fresh salmon washed down with Santa Rita tinto, all for the equivalent of two bucks!

Next morning we decided a day not involving buses was in order, so ambled along an endless beach, built a fire, cooked fish and quaffed more Santa Rita. The smooth sand also served as a road and locals sped by in their cabs, jeeps and cars.

Leaving Ancud early we bussed to Castro with its precarious, but picturesque, palafitos, then caught a second south to Quellon. With hindsight, we should have stopped there, but had read of a promising place and pushed on for that. Snow-capped peaks backdropped the undulating hills leading to Chaiguao, with rocky secluded bays and vibrantly painted wooden houses sprinkling the route. The glorious views came as a welcome distraction from the grim discomfort of a rollercoaster corrugated track so rough it threatened to dislodge teeth.

When the bus crossed a narrow bridge, turned around and pulled to a halt we realised we'd reached our destination, so stepped off, shouldered our packs, and started walking. According to the backpacker's bible, camping, horses and kayaks should have been available for hire, but aside from a few small houses, there was nothing in sight, so we just kept walking.

Before long the track degenerated into a muddy bog which Mrs Beeper waded through barefoot, whilst the rest of us took a slower route skirting around the thick slop. We came to an untamed sandy beach, but there was still no sign of a campsite or settlement. Spotting something indistinct way down the beach, Mr Beeper and I ditched our luggage, left the ladies lounging by the shoreline and headed off. Thirty minutes later all we had found was one man, one horse and one woman.

The horse was wild, the man seemed mute and terrified of two alien gringos and the women... well, naturally, she was sitting knitting alone on a beach in the middle of nowhere!

An hour later, from a solitary local, we discovered that, in fact, there were no kayaks, no horses for hire and no accommodation of any sort. And no more buses, for a whole week! By sheer chance and bad luck, we'd caught the only bus that served the remote spot. Worse still there was no shop and no food. We were led to a barn with a few meagre supplies and bought their entire stock... three Cokes, a Fanta and seven bags of mini biscuits!

Luckily, the owner's son had a pickup, so we secured a pricey ride back to Quellon. The unforgiving steel of the flatbed and dust combined to make our return journey an even more bruising ordeal, and as it was dusk, we had lost the views too.

Reflecting on the long, gruelling, wasted day, we realised what date it was... Friday 13th!!

From Quellon we took a car ferry through spectacular fjords of Canal Moraleda down to Puerto Aisen. A twenty-hour voyage with nowhere to sleep aside from rows of hard plastic seats. But sitting in the bow being lulled by the soft hiss of water caressing a steel hull, combined with the subtle deep throb of a big diesel engine more than compensated for the discomfort and sleep deprivation. Tucked out of the wind and warmed by sun I sat for hours as we navigated fathomless fiords squeezed between snow-dusted peaks. Killer whales cruised the surface, their tall dorsal fins projecting from dark waters as the pod patrolled past. The remote Chilean passage was also home to dolphins, seals and penguins, but we passed only one other boat.

From Aisen, we caught a bus to Coyhaique, and after a few days there decided to visit Parque Queulat. It was this decision that led to the spectacular eight-hour minibus ride slicing through Chile's giant Cheddar Gorge to Puyuhuapi.

TO CONTINUE SOUTH from Puyuhuapi, we first had to return to Coyhaique, so had the pleasure of taking the incredible trip for a second time. This time our driver managed to miss all the handful of vehicles we met and fortunately had a slightly more bearable musical taste...

WITH THE FOOTHILLS of the Andes forming a border with neighbouring Argentina, to reach Patagonia by road, one has to travel first through southern Argentina, which necessitates four border crossings. Although time-consuming and tedious, they ease the monotony of bus travel through endless expanses of wind-whipped Argentinian desert. With little to see apart from an occasional hardy fox or incongruous groups of lurid pink flamingos, hours pass slowly. So the chance of a leg stretch at a border is always welcome even if it's just to stand in line to await passport scrutiny.

With no direct buses and others fully booked we had to detour to make progress, which meant many hours waiting in dreary bus terminals. Dirty, spartan, concrete creations without colour and little concession to comfort. One such unwanted stop came in Rio Gallegos, some 200 miles north of Cape Horn, and it was here we had a bizarre brush with the law.

Seated on the floor playing cards around a backpack somehow upset a kiosk owner. First, this cheerless character complained we were blocking the aisle outside his little shop, which we weren't until he moved his display units up next to us. We pushed them back and kept playing, but he continued to hassle us and became abusive. There was little space in the busy terminal so we had to stay put. Then suddenly the police showed up and told us to stop playing or they would take us to the station!

Mrs Beepers command of Spanish was excellent but she couldn't reason with the keystone cops, so reluctantly we packed the offending cards away. Pacified, senor shopkeeper smugly lit a fat cigar, grinned at us and stood counting his bundle of cash. It was astounding the police responded to his complaint, but perhaps that was why he was counting his cash; because they were on his payroll.

Worse than the loss of the distraction of cards was having no music to listen to as my Walkmans batteries were dead. Instead, close by was a kids arcade game playing a tinny irritating tune on repeat every five seconds. We waited ten and a half hours in that packed dreary terminal, which meant I endured the maddening tune over seven thousand times!

NEXT MORNING I awoke around dawn cramped and freezing cold. Our bus was stationary at a desolate spot miles from habitation. It had broken down, and to make matters worse there was no toolkit onboard. After hours stuck beside the empty road, a truck stopped and the driver eventually managed to get our bus restarted.

Crossing back into Chile later that day, an officious border guard relieved passengers of all their food supplies, probably just to save on his shopping, so the final leg to Puerto Natales was a long hungry one.

On arrival, I noticed the Navimag ferry boat tied up and decided despite the endless buses, delays and discomforts we made the right decision in taking an overland route.

The journey through Argentina alone had entailed forty hours on four different buses, and twenty-four more spent waiting to catch them. But it had certainly been an adventure!

Spirits of Rapa Nui

LAN CHILE'S SANTIAGO to Isla de Pascua was possibly the planets most expensive domestic flight at just two bucks shy of 900 US dollars in 98. Despite being part of Chile, Easter Island is over 3700 km from the mainland making it one of the world's remotest inhabited islands. Tahiti is the second nearest landmass, but that's over 4000 km away. With a long-held fascination with the islands Moai it was a place I had to visit, so following the month-long meandering detour south, I found myself aboard their plane.

As Rapa Nui came into view, I thought our pilot had dozed off after the monotony of long hours above the empty South Pacific expanse as he flew right over the small island. A wide banking turn brought the aircraft around but now our approach was so low it seemed we would clip coastal rocks fronting the runway. We missed the massive rocks, used most of the airstrip, made a u-turn, and taxied back to the tiny airport. The diminutive terminal was so small that not all disembarking passengers could fit inside its single room, so the ensuing scramble for luggage became somewhat chaotic.

White garlands, hugs and smiles welcomed home returning islanders, as arriving tourists were greeted by friendly faced locals holding placards for guesthouses. I plumped for Ana Rapu, climbed into the back of a pickup, and was soon pitching my tent overlooking the bay behind her place in Hanga Roa.

MUCH INTRIGUE AND speculation surround Rapa Nui and its Moai as no written history of the island exists, only stories passed down through generations. Over the years many studies have been made and theories hypothesized, but nobody knows for certain all the secrets of Easter Island or its mysterious Moai.

Early next morning I was woken by the sound of my tents flysheet flapping in breeze. Odd, I thought sleepily, it had been fastened shut. Seconds later came the sound of the inner tent carefully being unzipped.

"Who's there?"

No reply.

I stuck my head outside, but saw no one. Mysterious place indeed!

OVER THE RHYTHMIC surge of Rapa Nui's surf relentlessly breaking over volcanic rock, I could hear the dawn chorus warming up. Cockerels started their strangled crowing and a lone dog was barking, but aside from the toll of a solitary bell, there were no sounds of human activity in Hanga Roa. Through the domed door of my tent, low-pitched buildings of the town stretched away, sprinkled with palms and overlooked by rolling hills. Gazing across the bay of Hanga Roa, home to all the islands 3000 inhabitants, I could just make out an imposing line of Moai standing above the surf.

Nearly 900 Moai dot the island and the tallest stretches to almost 10 metres high. Thought to have been created between 500 and 800 years ago, each was carved from tuff, compressed volcanic ash, at Rano Raraku crater, and then transported to ceremonial platforms around the island.

Historians first believed the 80 tonne statues were moved lying flat using ropes and wooden rollers, a theory reinforced by the sparsity of trees on the island. Current thinking suggests they were more likely walked standing upright, again with ropes, but utilising a rocking motion. It's thought rival clans erected Moai as ritualistic displays of wealth and power, and to honour their ancestors.

Much early history of Easter Island was lost due to the arrival of slave ships and missionaries in the 1860s and the subsequent conversion of islanders to Christianity. The combination of mass conscription of slaves and disease brought in by outsiders decimated the population. With the arrival of Christianity many artefacts, historical buildings and native artwork were destroyed as the traditional ways of Rapa Nui were outlawed.

LEAVING HANGA ROA I set out towards Rano Kau, a dormant volcanic crater dominating the south-western end of the island, skirting first around the runway that starts close to the rugged coast. Not a soul was in sight as I followed a rough track weaving upwards and on through the welcome, but short-lived shade of a eucalyptus grove. Under a roasting sun, the vague trail snaked onwards through low scrub until I reached the single-lane road that climbs to Orongo.

After a short spell on the smooth road, I left it behind and pushed on through coarse grasses towards the crater. Nearing the rim a great blast of warm air surged from the bowels two hundred metres below, then, a few steps further and the colossal crater lake was fully revealed.

Measuring a mile across, the circular lake is a mosaic of colour and dotted with islands and reeds, giving the impression of a gigantic vegetarian pizza! Looking south a massive bite is missing from the crater's towering rim, providing expansive views out to the Pacific. On the narrow land ridge between caldera and ocean, a small collection of squat stone buildings hug the ground; once ceremonial homes to the Birdmen cult.

With near vertical cliffs dropping a thousand feet to surf below the setting is spectacular. Legend has it that Birdmen held contests climbing down the sheer rock faces, then swimming out to the furthest islet to return with the season's first bird egg. Hundreds of petroglyphs cover rocks by the huddle of low round buildings, many depicting bird-headed human figures. It's believed the Birdmen cult thrived after the period when Moai stopped being made. Rapa Nui was once rich with colonies of seabirds which would have been an important food source to islanders.

My hike lasted seven long, hot hours and by the time

I got back to the tent, I'd decided to hire a bike to explore the rest of the island. Sadly, my budget wouldn't stretch to a motorbike as this was the start of a six-month trip, so I settled on a bicycle instead.

Within an hour of setting off next morning, I started to regret the decision. My suspension-less bike was laden with supplies and eight litres of water, I was wearing a backpack, the road was bumpy and there wasn't a scrap of shade in sight!

Red-dirt meandering track led along rugged coastline, past occasional toppled Moai, so my constant companion, aside from large hawks, was the soothing sound of surf. Rano Raraku, the Moai quarry, was my goal and when many hours later I spotted eucalyptus marking its foot, the sight came like an oasis in a desert. But the road taunted me and led on a long loop away from the trees before finally turning and heading for the much-needed shade.

Cheers and clapping greeted my weary arrival from Gert and Sandra, a couple I'd met the previous night, and stunned amazement (at my stupidity no doubt) from three tourists in a jeep! I guzzled a litre of water warm enough to brew tea, pitched my tent on the parched ground, and collapsed inside. Sometime later I climbed reluctantly back on the bike and pedalled standing, as my saddle brought pain, down to the sea for a soak behind the towering Moai at Tongariki.

Standing erect on a long raised rock ahu, the fifteen magnificent Moai of Tongariki were restored after a tsunami bowled them over in the 60s. Like most of the island's Moai, they face inland, watching over their creator's descendants. At Ahu Akivi there are seven that face the sea, maybe to help travellers find the island, or perhaps to guide returning fishermen ashore.

Strong chins and large broad noses make the long Maoi faces look proud, defiant and powerful. Some wear Pukao, or top knots, on their heads made from red scoria, which probably signifies the further importance of that carving.

It's difficult to convey feelings invoked standing near these impressive monoliths, but the isolated rugged setting, their imposing size, enigmatic expressions and the mystery that surrounds them is a potent combination.

BACK AT CAMP, thousands of ants had invaded my tent, so I suspended the food from a tree before shaking them out. But this proved a waste of time and marked the beginning of an all-night battle with the swarming insects. Sleep was impossible. After upending the floor and evicting every single one, they would soon invade en masse again, crawling all over my face and body, even up my nose. At first light, I gave up the fight and left.

Hiking from camp the startling sight of dozens of huge heads jutting from the hillside at crazy angles met my eyes. Looking like a pissed landscaper had planted them, Moai appeared to be sprouting from the ground. Some lay tilted back sunbathing, with only long faces visible, others stood tall and proud, head and shoulders exposed and rising to twenty feet.

Centuries of soil erosion had buried the bodies of these Moai leaving clusters of heads staring silently ahead, and the slopes of the long-dormant volcano are littered with them. Aside from parched grass little grows on the barren soil intensifying the powerful impression given by this surreal sight.

Further up I found mosaics of half-carved Moai laying where sculptors maximised use of available rock, resulting in the quarry slope resembling a giant jigsaw puzzle, with reclining Moai for pieces. Standing beside the bulk of a near-fully carved one lying attached to tuff, I marvelled at the skill, ingenuity and sheer effort needed to move and transport the massive statues across the island.

Climbing higher to the rim I gazed down to a reed-fringed lake, encircled by orange soil dotted with dozens of wild horses. Chiselled heads sprouted from fire-blackened crater slopes with others lying toppled face down in the dirt. Rano Raraku's hillsides are home to four hundred Moai, almost half of the island's total, creating a unique spectacle which perfectly combines the beauty and power of nature with the skilful endeavours of an ancient race of people.

Back at base, I dozed beneath a tree, tipped armies of ants from the tent, loaded my bike and set off again. This time, fortunately, an easy freewheel downhill over a smoother track due north to Anakena.

Palms, pale sand and placid blue waters met my eyes, along with another line of powerful-looking Moai; the islands best preserved or perhaps more likely, most recently carved. With limited camp spots available, I squeezed my one-man tent into a tiny gap between sharp thorn-bushes. A tight fit, but the view out was fantastic. After a refreshing swim and a snack, I felt ready to crash out when my new neighbours beckoned me over to their camp.

With beer coolers, stereo system and a large suspended table laid out with a feast, the camp was luxurious compared to mine. Lucia Tucki, the grandmother, thought I looked hungry so invited me to join her family for freshly speared fish. Having only crunched down a few crackers smeared with warm jam, I had plenty of space for fire-cooked fish! Despite limited communication the family's hospitality and generosity was incredible, and they shared food with me over the next couple of days.

Arriving later back at my tent, I found the flysheet unzipped, but a padlock on the inner tent had prevented further entry. When I'd told Ana in Hanga Roa about the first morning's tent experience, she asked what I had done the previous day. I relayed my visit to the line of nearest Moai and she told me I must have upset the spirits by walking on the ahu (ceremonial platform) at their base, so it was their retribution! Now that it had happened a second time I was thinking less of mysterious spirits and more about having my possessions stolen.

As darkness fell, I heard odd noises and thought someone was trying to take my bike, but without contact lenses, could see little but blurry shapes. Deciding that if I wanted to sleep in peace, the bicycle would have to come inside with me I dragged it in. I pulled the seat post out but couldn't remove the wheels, which left me covered in grease, supporting a saddleless bike, with no room to lie down. Desperate for sleep but unwilling to risk losing my rental deposit, I resorted to the only thing possible and balanced the bike above me!

Propping it between the handlebars and backpack, and using pans and my boots to gain height, I made just enough space to lie beneath it. But every time I shifted to get comfortable I had to lift the bike, roll over, and re-balance it above me again! For the second night in a row dawn couldn't come fast enough.

In the light of day, I decided the noises were probably due to my sleep-deprived imagination, but nevertheless, left the bike locked in the Conaf wardens hut later.

VISITING LUCIA'S FAMILY was Stephanie, a German lady who'd settled on the island and with her translating I relayed my nocturnal bicycle farce, much to everyone's amusement. Upsetting ancestor's spirits was again the consensus, and they told me many islanders believe ghosts and spirits inhabit Rapa Nui, and every cave, for example, has one, and people must seek permission before entry otherwise recriminations will follow!

Bidding the family farewell I set off for the ride back to Hanga Roa. Pedalling now felt a pleasure as I was carrying far less weight, having sold my tent, pans and stove to the Tucki's, and was no longer laden with so much water. Also, the final stretch into town was over sealed road for the first time in a week.

LATER, I WENT out with others staying at Ana's, and after drinks checked out the local disco advertised in spray-painted letters down the side of a small corrugated shack. Our visit was brief though, as inside the only reveller was the DJ, who also acted as barman!

Santiago bound again next morning, I wondered what delights a room at the Nuevo Hotel would bring this time. Surely it had to be more comfortable than my tent, hopefully with a lot less ants, and preferably no spirits present!

Flying with four wheels on the ground

TOWARDS THE NORTHERN end of the Andes, just inside the Bolivian border, lies the world's largest salt flat. Covering an area of over 4000 square miles, the Salar de Uyuni is the remains of a vast salt lake that once covered most of southwestern Bolivia. When the saline waters dried up, several salt pans were created, including the colossal Salar de Uyuni. Travelling north through Chile, the dazzling crystalline expanse of the Salar entices travellers with an opportunity for a three-day off-road adventure, ending in the small Bolivian town of Uyuni.

The thousand-mile journey from Santiago, up through Calama, aboard a Turibus coach passed with little bother, but rather more boredom. Much of the route follows Chile's wild uninhabited coast, providing endless expanses of sand and surf-lines to gaze at and let the mind wander. Inland, through harsh Atacama desert, mile-upon-mile of cactus fences lined the baked roads and turned my attention back to a book, or briefly to one of the low-budget action movies playing up front.

After a disrupted nights sleep due to bawling babies, coughing Chilenos and several stops, the second day drifted by in much the same fashion as the first. More desert, more pipelines, and more dry riverbeds. Interrupted only by random police checkpoints in the middle of nowhere, or poignant roadside shrines marking the scene of fatal crashes. Desert, dust and stifling heat were the day's constants. Along with the boredom!

The town was in total darkness when we arrived as apparently it was too early for the electricity to be turned on! But San Pedro de Atacama is only small, so it didn't take long to locate lodgings, with the help of a friendly local. The lack of light didn't help much though when it came to looking at rooms. Despite it being eight pm the power wouldn't be switched on for another hour, so I shone my torch around the budget room and tested the mattress. Both seemed bearable and were about as good as it got for a few thousand pesos, so I booked myself in.

Ros and Harriet, who I'd met on the bus, persuaded me to join them next morning on a horseback ride to nearby Death Valley, but my steed was the horse from Hell and sensing my inexperience wandered wherever he pleased. He stopped to eat at every opportunity, stubbornly refused to trot and turned back the moment the other riders disappeared around a corner. When, at last, we made it to Death Valley the damn thing rolled over in the sand, then ran away as I leapt off!

Sandwiched between the Andes and Pacific Ocean, the Atacama desert stretches 600 miles from Chile, into Bolivia and Southern Peru. Average annual rainfall here is just one millimetre, making it amongst the driest and most inhospitable places on the planet. When we weren't chasing the stroppy horse, we explored arid wind-sculpted canyons and barren rocky landscapes under a harsh, relentless sun.

After the reluctant horse got led home, I swapped the beast for a more comfortable and predictable ride aboard a Toyota out to Valle de la Luna.

Leaving San Pedro's dirt streets and adobe dwellings behind our Land Cruiser followed a rough track past abandoned mine workings and weird, twisted rock formations. At a broad white-crusted bowl we came to a halt, encircled by part-eroded salt mountains and huge wind-rippled sand dunes. Climbing a soft, shifting dune we trudged to the ridge and gazed over a strange lunar landscape below. Spectacular shadows, cast by the sinking sun, crept across a surreal moonscape until darkness engulfed the valley floor.

From the viewpoint of our giant body-hugging sand sofa, moonrise silhouetted craggy undulating ridges stretching before us as the psychedelic sounds of Pink Floyd drifted up from the Cruisers speakers. All too soon the time came to slide down the huge dune and head back to San Pedro. This time the lights were on in town, providing a brief window of opportunity to go in search of hot food before they shut the power off for the night!

Next morning we joined Colque Tours, for a three-day trip that would take us into Bolivia, and with luck, across the Salar de Uyuni. The Salar was two days drive away across the border, but as wet season had started, there was no guarantee when we got there it would be possible or safe to cross.

Delays at Chilean border control gave the chance to grab breakfast before our minibus set off along what would be the only paved road for three days, but even that lasted only a few hundred metres!

San Pedro de Atacama sits at an altitude of 2400m, but the dirt track leading from it climbed steadily through grand scale scenery. On the baked, rocky shores of Laguna Blanca, we reached the Bolivian border; comprising two rough buildings, a few guards, one lonely flag and little else. The location, by contrast, was spectacular, with the calm expanse of the lakes shallow waters mirroring mountain ranges stretching behind. Two volcanoes thrusting towards a blistering sun in cloudless blue sky dwarfed the squat buildings.

With backpacks now strapped on top of four-wheel-drive Toyota's, we set off with more leg space and fresh Bolivian stamps in passports. All day vague tracks led us higher, as the scenery continued to grow in scale and grandeur, and with no other vehicles in sight, our Land Cruisers looked lost amidst the vast landscape. Traversing huge gravel plains hemmed between mountains, the lead Toyota appeared ant-like on the surface, totally dwarfed by the dominating scale of its surroundings.

Reaching Laguna Verde, we watched as katabatic winds whipped up minerals in the lake, changing its blue waters to jade and lining the shore with masses of white, sticky, jelly-like foam. Later, we explored unearthly sites of geothermal activity with steaming vents and bubbling mud pools that spattered the unwary. Arriving at an alfresco thermal rock pool we shed clothes and lingered in the warm water, surrounded still by immense but near-barren scenery.

At Laguna Colorada, we made our final stop and left the Land Cruiser to explore its lakeshore. Crusty white salt formations ringed its rust-red waters, overlooked by rolling mountain ranges. Rare James flamingos dotted the lake, feeding on red algae that coloured its shallow waters, whilst groups of hardy alpaca scratched meagre livings along the shoreline.

Earlier, our Toyota's had climbed over a pass at 5000 metres, Laguna Colorada was only a few hundred metres lower, and the effects of altitude suddenly hit me. Having never experienced altitude sickness, I'd found it hard to believe stories that I'd heard, but now felt like I had aged fifty years. Short of breath and feeling exhausted, for a spell I doubted I could make the ten-minute walk back to a huddle of buildings where we were staying!

Once inside the simple bunk room, it seemed everyone was feeling the effects too, and even drinking mate de coca didn't help much. Mate seems to be the universal Andean cure for all sorts of ailments and is made by steeping leaves from coca plants in boiling water.

Surprisingly, the tiny community had a disco, and attendance was compulsory because when the music started every building lost its power and our room was plunged into darkness! When we wandered along for a look, seven of us doubled attendance in the tiny hall. Hidden behind huge twin speakers the DJ manning a tape deck soon whipped us into a frenzy with his fab collection of four cassettes! Meanwhile, lurking in shadows, a bunch of old men stood nursing small beers, staring in silence as gringo disco-fever engulfed the dance floor.

Day two got off to a slow start as everyone was struggling with altitude sickness, and most had endured a sleepless night with splitting headaches whilst feeling sick. Back aboard the vehicles, more incredible vistas helped distract from how we were all feeling.

Our mini-convoy pushed on through vast empty landscapes, passing more lagunas inhabited by flocks of incongruous looking flamingos. Aside from the twin Toyota, we saw no other vehicles all day, and apart from the flamingos and an occasional solitary llama, there were little other signs of life.

We stopped to climb an improbably balanced tree-like rock sprouting from the barren plain, and later, by a poorly camouflaged army camp for passport scrutiny and a short interrogation from the commandant.

As we were about to leave the base, a parade ground band burst into life and struck up the national anthem. Soldiers snapped to rather slack attention as two more rushed to the battlement, then trained rifles on imaginary targets out in the void beyond!

Later, the tiny community of Manica provided our

posse with beds for the second night. Home to only a handful of families and flocks of spitting llama, the isolated collection of tumbledown dwellings surprisingly had its own basketball court. We tried to play, but local kids ran rings around us as we struggled to get enough oxygen from the thin air.

Sometime after leaving Manica behind next morning, we started to follow a rough track along the shore of the Salar, until both drivers stopped for no apparent reason. They jumped out and began collecting bundles of something resembling heather, and bringing back armfuls, stuffed it into the front grilles before climbing back into their seats. The low tech solution was intended to keep salt out of the engines but would do little to aid cooling.

A simple road sign appeared, the first in days, pointing at right angles into an endless lake. Just above water-level, a stony finger-like track jutted out, and we turned onto that. The narrow track was in poor condition and we dropped into ever-deeper water holes, and then, after less than half a mile, the rudimentary road ended. Ahead, a calm sea stretched to infinity, and into that, we drove!

It felt surreal. In front of us was only water and vast blue sky scattered with clouds, nothing else. The smooth water acted as a giant mirror and merged seamlessly with the sky, so there was no horizon. With no points of reference, it looked like we were driving off the edge of the world.

Our drivers spread apart to keep spray down and

accelerated into an endless expanse of still water. With no horizon and the glassy surface reflecting the huge sky, our world became one of shimmering shades of blue and white, with shards of silvery spray thrown up by the tyres.

As minutes, then hours slipped by in comfort across the smooth salt crust and we gazed at unchanging mirrored sky around us, it was easy to imagine we were flying. When a mountain range in the far distance first came into hazy view, it would appear like a great rip in the sky, giving glimpses into another world. Alien rocky colours did not exist in the universe we'd been flying through.

WE'D BEEN TRAVELLING all morning when our Toyota started to sputter, and one look at the drivers face confirmed he wasn't fooling about. Moments later its engine died and wouldn't restart. We stepped out, happy to stretch and breathe fresh air, but more than a little concerned we'd just broken down in the middle of the world's largest salt flat.

On board was neither toolkit nor radio, so we had no communication with the lead vehicle which hadn't been seen for some time. After trying to dry the engine our drivers were stumped, so faced with few alternatives we attempted to bump start it! Under a fierce sun the six of us tried to push our laden Land Cruiser over flat salt pan, but of course it was futile, so after that, all we could do was hope the others came back to find us. With time to kill, we splashed around in the warm shallow water, snapped silly photos and waited to be rescued.

Below three inches of water, a rough crystalline mosaic of hexagonal shapes made up the salt crust, melting into an immense mirror encircling us. It turned out we had been lucky and broken down not far from an island due to be our lunch spot, so when we failed to show the others came back to search for us.

The Land Cruiser would still not fire up, so they tried a tow-start and thinking less weight would help, told our six friends to hop out. As both Toyota's disappeared into the distance, the now dozen stranded gringos could do nothing but watch, and start walking after them!

When at last they got the vehicle started, they came back for us, and soon we were enjoying lunch on Isle de Pescadores. Now, instead of being surrounded by water, we sat encircled by hundreds of giant cacti on the strange isolated island. Standing twenty feet tall, green and silvery-brown cacti sprouted between rocks in every direction. The remote oasis even had a resident gardener, paid by the state to tend the spiky plants, who lived at the lonely spot along with his dog.

Hours later we spotted a small building which at first sight appeared to be floating. Hotel del Sol turned out to be constructed almost entirely out of salt blocks hacked from the Salar's crust. Walls, pillars, floors and even some furniture were all made from salt. Surrounded by the Salar's flooded silken surface, views from every room were sublime. Fifteen bucks was the price for a night, and business must have been booming as they were building a second structure alongside the first.

After eight hours of driving, we finally crossed the salt flat and arrived in Uyuni. In all that time we had seen perhaps four or five other off-road vehicles, plus surprisingly two packed buses.

Arriving in Uyuni was like stepping back in time, with primitive street scenes reminiscent of rural China. Rows of huddled traders squatted behind wooden handcarts, the women wrapped in layers of shawls and wearing black bowler hats. Filthy water had flooded the rough potholed streets, and we learnt we were the first group for days who'd been able to make the long crossing.

But by the look of the waterlogged streets and a brooding bank of approaching storm clouds, it seemed it could well be a challenge to leave again!

Death Road, El Diablo and Dynamite

OUR SHOPPING LIST was short:

Alcohol.

Coca.

Dynamite!

An unlikely, but lethal cocktail.

It shouldn't have been possible for a bunch of gringo tourists with barely a command of Spanish between us to be shopping for sticks of dynamite, but this was South America, and with grubby Boliviano banknotes in pockets, no problema!

Kitted out in yellow macs and plastic hard hats we were perusing an early market in Potosi, a mining town high in the Andes, buying gifts for miners. The shopping list may have been short, but this was the start of what would turn out to be a long day. A day spent underground.

Home to prowling packs of hungry street dogs the ramshackle market consisted of a rough collection of blue corrugated tin kiosks and coloured tarps. Bowler-hatted women squatted beside giant sacks of coca, dispensing the dried narcotic leaves in plastic bags. The tiny shacks selling booze and dynamite also happily accepted our dinero, so with the shopping sorted we jumped aboard two jeeps and set off in a torrential downpour.

Wet season had only just started, but already roads resembled rivers, and at an altitude of 4500 metres above sea level, our breathing became as laboured as the jeeps progress up the steep incline. At the top, we pulled to a halt and spilt out into the surrounding puddles, then milled around the mine entrance whilst Julio wandered off to collect torches.

A sudden warning shout gave us just enough time to jump from the path of an ore truck that burst from the tunnel, then barrelled past spraying muddy water. Clinging to the back were two young lads, both black from head to toe. Wearing jeans, t-shirts and trainers, their ill-fitting hard hats were the only concession to safety.

With the laden truck passed we followed steel tracks into a narrow mine-shaft and in moments darkness engulfed us. Sloshing single file through muddy underfoot slop our lamps gave just enough light to make out a few shapes moving ahead. Low wooden beams made progress slow, as did negotiating the hazardous, steep, slippery shafts between levels.

The low tunnels had been laboriously carved from rock by hand, creating just enough space to work and we flattened ourselves to the sides as miners struggled past bearing thirty-kilo ore sacks on their backs. Every day they made at least forty such trips, but after just one looked shattered, dripping with sweat and gasping for breath.

With punishing backbreaking labour, primitive working conditions and few concessions to safety it's little wonder life expectancy of a miner is as low as ten years. Officially, if they make it to sixty, or have thirty percent lung cancer they can retire. The oldest miner working was forty-eight, but the youngest was just twelve years old.

To survive the hardship and gruelling work, many miners chew wads of coca leaves, which act as a stimulant and help suppress hunger. With large balls of leaves packed inside mouths, their black faces bore pink stretched bulges protruding from cheeks.

SPANIARDS FOUNDED THE city in 1545 when they discovered old Indian mine workings, and by early seventeenth century Potosi had become the biggest city in the Americas due to the riches excavated there. Along with silver, copper and lead were also mined, but in the 1980s reserves became so depleted that the mine shut down. Nowadays a small cooperative of hopeful miners still works the mine, in conditions that have hardly changed in centuries.

We descended deeper into the labyrinth, meeting miners and handing out bottles of booze, coca leaves or sticks of dynamite. By chance, it was a workers fiesta, a day of celebration and many appeared to be doing little apart from drinking, but it remained unclear why they were still underground.

Conditions were grim. There was no power, so consequently no light. No ventilation system meant no fresh air, and there were neither stairs nor ladders, let alone lifts. Rough steps had been hacked into the rock but had worn rounded and become polished over time making them treacherously slippery.

Apart from compressed air power tools at the vein face, everything was done by hand. Workers pushed or pulled the heavy steel carts and even winches were operated by muscle power alone. Everything we saw was primitive and archaic. Tools were basic and in short supply, the ore trucks old and tired, and their hand winches didn't even have bearings.

With no light, no space, no air and a sensation of a huge weight of mountain bearing down, I started to find the experience oppressive. But I was just a temporary visitor, and one hoping to leave soon. These men had to work here. Every day. And work hard.

The unusual underground adventure then took on a whole new bizarre dimension.

Squeezed inside a small side cave, we sat around a large statue of the Devil listening to an ex-leader of the Sendero Luminoso (Shining Path) toast Bolivia, the mine, Potosi and anything else he could think of as he got steadily more pissed!

It was surreal; eight gringos hunched deep underground with Bolivian miners drinking moonshine, in front of a Devil effigy adorned with bunting, wearing wellies and sporting a massive penis!

The foul tasting booze was lethal, but the endless rounds of shots and toasts went on and on. Every time the plastic bottle had been emptied another would be pulled from behind the horny pointy-eared Devil.

Finally, we escaped and left El Diablo and the dingy claustrophobic cavern, all much worse for wear, and started the now even more challenging climb to the surface and outside world.

Seven and a half hours after first entering the mine I breathed fresh air again. It was a relief to be above ground once more, and I'd never been so pleased to see a wet, miserable, grey day.

FROM POTOSI, WE headed to La Paz, the world's highest capital, perched at 3640 metres above sea level. Carnival had started so we wanted to join the fun. After several false starts and delays, our bus departed an hour late, and with bumpy unmade roads and river crossings, as usual comfort wasn't high. But with spectacular scenery, snaking Andean passes, llamas, raging swollen rivers and lush floodplains, the journey was a visual feast.

Stopping at a rough-looking roadside cafe in Chapakoota, my spoon encountered something solid in the thin broth and I fished a chicken claw from the bottom of my bowl. I set it aside, but as we left, I'm sure I saw it get put back in the pot!

Arriving in La Paz eight hours later, seemed like entering another world. Traffic was chaotic, with four or five vague lanes crammed together in each direction. Cabs, buses, micros and minibuses all jostled for position and a chance to gain a few metres. It was street warfare as they darted in and out of non-existent gaps with total disregard for anyone or anything else.

A car horn cacophony made up the city soundtrack and crossing the main street was best avoided if possible. Several times in narrow side-streets buses grazed my back as I slalomed around the melee of traders and an endless tide of people.

With Carnival in full swing, the Prado resembled a riot zone and became a risky place for pale-faced gringos to linger, so we bought foam face masks and water pistols and went to war!

With hordes of people on the street nobody seemed safe, and within minutes we were plastered in spray foam and soaked to the skin. Palm-sized water-bomb balloons fell like monsoon rain, whilst kids manned water cannons and hoses high on roofs. Families waited in ambush, heavily armed with buckets, water-bombs, confetti and foam. Even dancers in the street processions came prepared, and a foam attack could result in a bludgeoning from a sand-filled truncheon!

After hours of fun our masks had fallen apart making us more obvious targets, so we jumped on a bus and escaped back towards the hostel. As our bus crawled through the crowds, I witnessed an old women take a direct hit from a balcony high above. A whole bucket of water landed on her head, leaving her soaked and looking bewildered. The madness continued for days and it wasn't safe to venture out for long unless you didn't mind coming back drenched yet again.

After a week or so, I left La Paz and headed for the chilled out village of Coroico, which entailed a four-hour trip through spectacular scenery. It also meant I had to risk being a bus passenger on the Death Road.

Also known as the Yungas road, this infamous track was cut from mountainside in the 30s by Paraguayan prisoners. It stretches almost seventy kilometres and snakes its way up to 4650 metres before descending to 1200 at Coroico. From the crumbling edge of its unmade road, sheer drops plunge thousands of feet to rainforest below. There are no barriers.

Just a few years ago it was estimated between two and three hundred people crashed to their deaths over the side every year. In 1983 over a hundred people died in one accident alone when an overcrowded bus veered off the road. Near vertical cliffs and the colossal drops prevent vehicles or bodies ever being recovered.

Wet conditions, hairpin bends, rockfalls and mud-slides add further danger to traversing this notorious narrow dirt track. The treacherous conditions and horrific annual death toll have earned it the reputation of being the world's most dangerous road.

The journey was nerve-wracking, especially when we needed to squeeze past an oncoming vehicle. With a rock face on one side and a precipice the other, our bus literally had to scrape by, with wheels only inches from the edge. It was a slow, anxious and risky manoeuvre every time.

Seated by a window on the left side, often I couldn't see anything of the road, only jungle far below. In other places wooden crosses and little shrines lined the route marking many spots where people had lost their lives.

Midway, sudden crashing sounds brought gasps and cries of alarm, but it was only cascading torrents pounding the roof as we'd just driven under a waterfall! When we made it safely to Coroico, our driver was rewarded with a round of applause.

AFTER THE FRANTIC pace of La Paz, Coroico came as a total contrast. No traffic, no noise, no pollution. Instead, exotic bird calls penetrating jungle, darting hummingbirds, huge butterflies and clean fresh air.

The sleepy village was a perfect antidote to the madness of the capital and the anxious moments of being a passenger on Death Road. The only downside was that in order to move on in a few days time, I would probably first have to return to La Paz.

And risk the Death Road a second time!

Birthplace of the Sun, Bolivian Armada and a Brown Snouted Peruvian Pig

THE ROAD TO Rurrenabaque was underwater. Reports had filtered back of vehicles being swept away by seasonal floods, along with stories of buses being stranded for days. From Coroico the journey generally took less than a day, but now if you were lucky enough to make it through, it was more likely to take three.

With little realistic hope of reaching Rurrenabaque, I decided to return to La Paz but heard the Death Road had yet again been blocked by a landslide. A day later when the notorious route reopened, I wasted no time in catching a bus back to the capital. Having survived the journey once, my second trip seemed less intense, until our driver left the risky pass behind and reached long sweeping bends approaching La Paz. With utter disregard for passenger safety, he sped recklessly over the barrier-less tarmac mountain road in torrential rain. I had glanced at the tyres whilst waiting to board, which were beyond bald with chunks of sidewall missing, so it seemed a minor miracle when we made it back to the madness of the city's chaotic streets.

One day back in La Paz was enough, and I left the Bolivian capital behind in more pouring rain, to the disturbing sight of distraught backpacker who'd just had her pack stolen in the bus station. With corrupt officials and opportunist thieves about, I usually chained my backpack to the bus, or sometimes two packs together. It was always a performance but ensured peace of mind on long road trips.

TRAVELLING AGAIN WITH friends I first met in Chile, our route towards Peru led us to Copacabana on the shores of sparkling Lake Titicaca. According to ancient Andean belief, the expansive lake was the birthplace of the sun. Ironically, it's also home to Bolivia's landlocked navy.

Since losing their coastline to Chile in a war almost 150 years ago, the Bolivian Armada can now only patrol the lake and parts of the Amazon river. The tiny naval base maintained at Copacabana had a sad-looking fleet that seemed to consist of a solitary rowing boat and five colourful kayaks lying forlornly on the shore!

Lake Titicaca is the highest commercially navigable body of water in the world, at an altitude of over 3800m, and contains several sizeable islands. The largest, Isla del Sol, was the spot once worshipped as the birthplace of the sun, and also of the first two Inca's.

We spent a night on the island and our hillside hostel boasted the first comfortable bed I'd found after three months in South America, plus possibly the best view from a toilet window anywhere in the world! We hiked for hours to find the Inca ruins but failed to find them, only getting redder and thirstier under a fierce sun.

Back on the mainland, we ate bland fried fish claimed to be lake trout and watched bemused as cars and buses got blessed on the cobblestones outside Copacabana's impressive cathedral.

Inside the grand white building, we found a lavish gilt altar, intricate silverwork and walls adorned with fine art. The opulent interior also housed a rather masculine dark-skinned statue of the Virgin of the Lake, patron saint of Bolivia. But the riches contained within the cathedral seemed at complete odds with the region's poverty, as outside, homeless Indians begged in the street.

Leaving the lakeside town behind we headed for the border wedged inside another ageing overcrowded bus. The usual long-winded farcical crossing followed, with endless paperwork, chaotic queues and exit stamps. Then came a short walk to the Peruvian side where the whole protracted procedure started again.

Instead of anticipated problems entering Peru, we were greeted by blaring music, naked calendar girls on the walls and casually dressed border officials selling bootleg cassette tapes on the side!

With fresh Peruvian ink in our passports, we jumped back aboard the bus and continued on to Puno where we checked into a small friendly hostel close to the plaza.

FROM PUNO A two-day boat trip took us back onto the placid blue waters of Titicaca, steering first for Uros. This collection of miniature floating islands are man-made from six foot thick bundles of totora reed. The Uru people bind and weave these together, then anchor them with ropes to the lakebed. Underfoot the soft reeds felt spongy and sinky, making it easy to get a soaked boot and sock. As the reeds gradually rot they have to be regularly replenished with newly cut reeds laid on top. The islands home a handful of families in simple reed huts, who eke livings harvesting the lake supplemented by selling handicrafts to visiting tourists.

From Uros, we motored to Taquile where a nights stay came included in the ten dollar tour price. Our boat was met by a gaggle of bowler-hatted hostesses looking somewhat apprehensive at the prospect of having gringos for guests. As the island had no official accommodation everyone was led away in different directions.

We followed our silent guide along a pebbly beach and up through fields of quinoa to a tumbledown building. There was no sign of people, but the hovel came with chickens, a donkey, a lively black kitten and one large brown nosed pig. Our room had no electricity, no windows and no mattress, but there was an alfresco toilet nearby. Comprising three stone walls and a hole in the ground, the crumbling structure had neither roof nor door, but ever-present below the hole was the large brown snout of a hungry pig!

Our hostess had still not uttered a single word, she

just pointed to the room and scuttled away, leaving us to wonder if we would get any lunch. Nosing around I found her preparing food, so before long we were sipping lukewarm soup and giving inedible crunchy rice to the grateful chickens. We couldn't offend her by returning half full plates, but neither could we risk being seen feeding it to the foul, as she was our only food source on the small island!

Later, after several hours exploring Inca ruins, climbing endless rock steps and admiring sublime views over the lake at sundown, we returned to more under-heated soup and crunchy rice. Perhaps, we reasoned, she didn't like gringos, and it was a simple ploy to save cash and get her chooks fed for free!

One night in the chilly room lying on a stack of wooden slats under a mound of itchy blankets was one too many, so in the morning we set off for Amantani. Overnight storms had whipped up the lake, and any remaining drowsiness soon disappeared during the rollercoaster ride, but our overloaded boat made it across the choppy waters without incident and dropped us on the island's stony shores.

On Amantani we went in search of Inca cola and fully cooked food, then kicked a football around with kids in its square, surrounded by crumbling adobe buildings. The small island appeared untouched by time, with all its Quechuan inhabitants still in traditional clothing. Men wore simple black and white but sported knitted red-patterned tasselled hats, with the women all wrapped in brightly coloured shawls and skirts topped with pom-pom straw hats or black bowlers. Hoping to snap some stealthy candid shots of the colourful islanders, the sight of my Sigma zoom lens was met with a scowl or a swiftly repositioned bowler hat!

By late afternoon we were back on the mainland, chilling out in our hostel and contemplating the morning's train to Cusco and the Sacred Valley.

IN SOUTH AMERICA, you never really know when a ticket office will open, even in the rare event of a sign advertising an opening time. So it's advisable to turn up early, which is what we did. However, despite the station office supposedly unlocking its doors at seven, no staff bothered to show up for a further hour. With only six people ahead of us in the queue, we thought the wait would be short inside the cramped room but endured another hour before our turn arrived at the window. For each western traveller, every passport detail was painstakingly recorded, making the laborious process way too slow. But finally, clutching Inca class train tickets, we left the office.

A sudden violent lurch spat baggage from the tiny racks onto heads and laps below, annoyingly also smashing a bottle of vodka standing in readiness for the long trip. But we were off!

The next twelve hours passed in a blur of card games and cramped limbs, thanks to being hemmed in by backpacks, passengers and locals luggage. Steel rail tracks took us across the altiplano past remote villages with rough adobe structures and herds of strutting white llama. Stops at filthy flooded stations gave an opportunity to buy hot snacks from trackside vendors but could be a gamble as you never knew what you were buying and food hygiene was unheard of. In the backstreet markets of La Paz, it was even possible to purchase a llama fetus! But these were not intended for the table, instead, to bury under your house for luck!

Mid-afternoon our train pulled to a halt in the middle of nowhere, and a long delay ensued. The surrounding scenery was spectacular as the tracks ran parallel to the snow-capped Andes, so most passengers climbed down into the lush grass to stretch legs and breathe mountain air. A rumour circulated that the train had hit someone and they had lost a leg, which seemed highly unlikely out here. We never discovered the truth, but after a lengthy stop our driver set off again.

Approaching a built-up area after dusk abruptly all the carriage lights went out, and we travelled on in total darkness. A Peruvian passenger told us they had been switched off to prevent kids from stoning the passing train! They never came back on again so disembarking in Cusco was chaotic as we scrambled to collect backpacks and belongings together by torch and candlelight.

A horde of hoteliers waiting on the crowded platform hustled and cajoled us, all eager to get their hands on our dinero. We squeezed into a taxi, drove through darkened streets, clambered out then walked on through narrow, dimly lit, back alleys. Ten minutes later we arrived at Mirador del Inka, a rundown but spacious hillside hostel which had once been a hippy commune and came complete with a resident parrot.

Next morning gazing from its balcony, a terracotta roof-tiled sprawl of the ancient Inca capital spread below me, backdropped by rolling green mountain ranges. Giant letters carved into the slopes read Viva El Peru Glorioso.

Long Live Glorious Peru!

Hiking the Inca Trail

A GAPING HOLE in the road brought our minibus to an abrupt halt. Ten feet below the raging brown waters of Rio Urubamba churned and boiled around a collapsed mass of boulders and soil. The whole width of the road ahead had disappeared into the flood-torn river, leaving a forty-foot long section missing. With a dry stone wall on the other side, there was no way our driver could squeeze by, so we unloaded supplies and backpacks then carried them past the still crumbling collapse. Back in my hostel, I'd heard trekkers horror stories of hiking knee deep in mud, and our inauspicious start didn't fill me with confidence that the Inca trail would have improved much.

Once everything had been reloaded and strapped onto a second vehicle we set off again, and this time our minibus made it all the way to the drop-off. We donned shorts, shouldered our packs and set off on the four-day hike.

Instead of slogging through mud we sloshed through shallow water at first. The route running like a stream, resulting in soggy boots and socks from the outset. Ronnie, our guide, had set off at a fast pace, and soon the group was strung over a distance with helper

Horatio bringing up the rear. With his short legs and little shoulder satchel, he resembled a reluctant schoolboy trotting behind!

After a short climb, the track levelled a little, following a raging river course eating into the valley floor below. Spiky agave and cacti marked our way as the narrow path climbed higher up a hillside. Walking in alternate showers and sunshine, brightly coloured rain ponchos dotted the green landscape draped over backpacks and people.

After stopping for a rather odd lunchtime snack combining fruit with corn, fried cauliflower, cheese and salad, we got back on the trail and left the river behind. Descending a steep gorge, the track crossed a treacherous log bridge above another wild brown torrent, before climbing an exposed plain surrounded by breathtaking scenery. Here we encountered the first Inca ruins, a large settlement hunched into the hillside and blending so well with surrounding rock that nobody noticed it for a while.

Throughout the afternoon the track climbed with little respite, passing isolated dry stone villages inhabited by ragged collections of chickens and semi-wild dogs with scruffy infants running barefoot between them.

It was late afternoon when we reached Huayllabamba camp and with our tents already pitched, it was time to rest or play cards whilst the guides prepared dinner. With daylight fading, we feasted on more conventional chicken and rice by flickering candlelight before retiring to chilly and rather leaky tents.

I'd hoped to hike the Inca trail independently, but a recent spate of robberies, including one where a backpacker got shot, put me off the idea. But next morning with an obvious route leading from camp I set off at the front, giving a sense of exploring rather than just following. We trudged steadily up relentless incline accompanied by intermittent rain, but then I started to feel unwell. All morning both my stomach and the weather deteriorated, and when three hours later we stopped for a break I had to run for the toilet.

Our camp at Huayllabamba had been at 3000 metres, but despite the near-constant uphill path we still had a long way to go to reach the pass above us at 4200. Pushing on in persistent rain we climbed rough muddy trails through cloud-forest and rugged mountain scenery, but all the time my backpack was becoming heavier as my strength began to desert me.

Before long I was weaving unsteadily along the rock-strewn track, with Shie walking close behind to catch me if I collapsed off the side. I was feeling terrible and had uncontrollable trots to contend with. With no cover in sight on the exposed mountainside, all I could do was slither a few feet from the path to squat like a nesting bird in my poncho!

Somehow I made it up to the pass at Warmiwanussca but was too ill to take much pleasure in the incredible mountain scenery. From the high pass, the trail descended at last, but the endless stone steps were running with water as the rain had still not let up.

Lush vegetation, rugged mountains and cascading falls surrounded us but I felt so weak that I wanted the trek to be over. After a tough few hours descending steps, we reached camp two at Pacasmayo. It was cold, covered in thick mud but at least had a proper sit-down toilet.

My stomach problems had worsened and was now throwing up as well. I spent a long uncomfortable night shivering by a log fire in the porter's shelter, in between frantic trips to the toilet.

Day three dawned much brighter, but I felt shattered and again the trail started with a gruelling ascent. The constant stone steps were a real struggle as I had little energy left and had barely slept. But halfway up the pass, the sun came out, and we sat amongst ancient Inca stonework surrounded by spectacular Andean scenery. With my stomach now beyond empty and the warmth of sunlight on my face, I began to feel slightly better.

The track climbed higher taking us to a 4000-metre pass at Runcuracy, but the weather had closed in again and we hiked enshrouded by swirling cloud. Often the slope plunged away from the trail, but we could see nothing of the drop below as we followed a path blindly into clouds. Later we reached the stone ruins of Sayacmarca, once a control point for trade carried in Inca times, now a place for weary hikers to take a welcome break.

From the ruins, an incredible route led through cloud-forest along a track hacked from mountainside and on through a natural rock tunnel. After eight long hours, we reached our last stop and slumped relieved into the hostel's seats.

With everyone enjoying celebratory beers, I had to settle for a hot cup of mate de coca to help my stomach bug. But the small bowl of boiled rice I ate slowly seemed like a feast after having no food for over a day! Following a few rounds of Israeli whist we crashed out early on the floor, under a dry roof for the first time in days.

Dawn of day four brought yet more rain as we hiked in hope towards the Sun Gate. An hour and a half later the sun still hadn't showed as we peered down to a rather dreary first glimpse of mystical Machu Picchu. Through cloud and drizzle the ruins seemed an anticlimax after all our effort, but as we drew closer, the skies cleared revealing the magnitude of the lost city and the splendour of its remote setting. Our early dawn start paid off, and we had the ancient Inca ruins almost to ourselves.

MACHU PICCHU IS thought to have been built in the fifteenth century and contains two hundred structures, made from precisely cut stone fitted perfectly together without mortar. In places, it would be impossible to slide a knife blade between the heavy blocks of stone. At its heart, a huge slab of carved granite called the Intihuatana rises from a terraced pyramid, which was possibly a sundial or for astronomical purposes, used in religious and spiritual ceremonies.

Conquistadors never found the isolated site meaning much of it is well preserved, and after Incas abandoned the citadel Machu Picchu lay hidden for hundreds of years. It wasn't until 1911 that American explorer and archaeologist Hiram Bingham discovered the ruins.

Although a lot of mystery remains around the lost city, it's thought Machu Picchu was perhaps once a summer retreat for rulers or royalty from nearby Cuzco, capital of the great Inca empire.

From its rise in the 11th century, the Inca civilisation became one of the worlds greatest planned societies as they conquered enormous territories, imposing State rule and Quechua language over the Indian population. By harnessing localised expertise and skill in construction, metalworking and textiles, rulers organised families into larger working groups, forging a rapidly advancing civilisation.

The Inca flourished until Spaniards arrived from the north in the early 1500s. During that period, the once powerful empire had been decimated by the spread of smallpox from Central America and been divided by war. Driven by greed and the prospect of great wealth and treasures, the invaders used superior tactics and weaponry to overthrow a weakened empire.

BEHIND MACHU PICCHU lies the peak of Huayna Picchu, and I'd heard it was possible to get the top. So despite protesting leg muscles and lack of energy I had to attempt the climb it as it didn't seem likely I would visit

Peru again. I couldn't persuade anyone else to join me though as they all felt too tired!

The ascent turned out to be the hardest and steepest part of the trek but most rewarding. Wet slabs of rock and near vertical sections meant I had to climb using my hands, then nearing the top, I squeezed through a narrow tunnel before emerging onto the exposed summit.

Gazing down from a warm slab of rock the majestic spectacle of Machu Picchu spread seven hundred metres below. Above, was clear blue sky and blazing sun as I shared the summit with four people and a small flight of butterflies. In an instant, all the discomforts of my gruelling trek faded away.

From Huayna Picchu, the slope plunged in every direction. Eleven hundred metres below the swollen brown waters of Rio Urubamba snaked through the valley floor. Rugged verdant ridges of the Andes surrounded the peak with the stone terraced Inca citadel of Machu Picchu nestled in the middle. It's little wonder Spaniards never found the spectacular remote location, but it's astonishing it was settled in the first place. The scale and skill of construction in the challenging topography defy belief.

Descending from the summit was also a challenge as my route had countless flights of steep short steps. Their treaders weren't deep enough to fit a boot on, so had to be carefully negotiated sideways leaning into the slope.

With a train to catch from Aguas Calientes, I re-joined my friends, and we left the lost city behind, descending yet more steps down into the valley. Soon we reached the banks of the Urubamba, which had become a wild cauldron of boiling water smashing over huge boulders and sending up heavy clouds of spray.

The station was in chaos as the flood-torn river had caused a landslide which blocked the track cutting off our train. After a long and uncertain wait, an overcrowded train pulled in, and the fight was on to climb aboard. Inside our carriage was a crush of people impossible to count, wedged standing together, with no room to move.

We endured an hour before prising ourselves from the compartment and climbing into a waiting minibus.

Moments later I was heading for Cusco, looking forward to a much-needed shower, quickly followed by several large meals, then my comfy dry mattress!

Bandits, Breakdowns, Condors and a Didgeridoo

THE RAPID-FIRE RACKET of a thousand firecrackers exploding over pounding bombo drums, trombones and tubas announced the military parade's arrival into the plaza. First into view stomped the marching band, followed by a squad of saluting soldiers. With camouflaged faces, it was obvious they were Commandos, because large letters on their headbands declared so! In their footsteps, a platoon of squaddies goose-stepped past the stand of assembled dignitaries and smartly dressed officials. Next came a patrol of police officers plodding proudly along in step. Hundreds more pairs of polished boots paraded past, then behind them rolled heavy artillery guns. Bringing up the rear, was some massive earthmoving equipment, which just seemed to have tagged along for a jolly.

Passing over cobblestones in the shadow of the plaza's grand colonial architecture the entire procession looked incongruous, especially with the inclusion of a large yellow earthmover at the back!

Seated close to a fountain at the centre of Cusco's crowded main square an Indian family of five surrounded me, all intent on selling me something as I stared in disbelief at the passing Sunday parade.

"Choomper senor? Compra mi. Muy barato, senor! Compra mi."

Jumpers, jewellery, carved gourds and weavings. Belts, ceramics, cigarettes, postcards and Chiclets. The array of choice was as wide and colourful as the persistent and ever-present indigenous street sellers.

My two-week stay in the ancient Inca capital was coming to a close, and I wasn't looking forward to the next leg, an overnight bus trip to Arequipa. In parts of Peru, buses had been held up at gunpoint by the Shining Path who sometimes shot at the bus to force it to stop. Some regions had become out of bounds to travellers due to the high risk of a holdup. The route to Arequipa was reputedly safe to travel, but buses only ran at night making the journey much riskier.

As usual, several vendors clambered aboard to offer their wares, including one wild-eyed Indian who spent long minutes making a speech blessing the bus and passengers against bandits, breakdowns and bad crashes. He then stuck a six-inch nail up each nostril, sold a few bags of boiled sweets and buggered off!

The fifteen-hour ride lived up to its reputation as being a bone rattler, and it felt like I had finally fallen asleep when we pulled into the bus terminal. But I came round to the spectacular sight of snow-capped El Misti volcano which appeared to be floating on a cloud above the squat urban sprawl of Arequipa.

The mad blessing must have worked as we made it past the bandits, avoided accidents and didn't break down, but during the night one passenger's daypack had disappeared. Hoping I would doze off, mine had been attached by dog chain to my wrist, and the precaution paid off, but she had lost some important possessions.

Amidst Arequipa's dusty streets lies Santa Catalina Convent, a miniature self-contained city within a city, once home to 450 nuns, who lived there in complete seclusion. Founded over 500 years ago the monastery was shrouded in secrecy until it opened its doors in the seventies. Now the cobbled streets and once silent corridors are a peaceful place to wander and admire its fine colonial architecture.

Arequipa, like most Peruvian towns, has its own Plaza de Armas, but this one was actually manned by a uniformed guard. Dressed like a bellhop boy, this comical character spent his days blowing a whistle and gesticulating wildly at anyone who dared sit on the walls of the fountain or wander onto the grass. The massive cone of El Misti volcano backdropped the manicured parade square, which was also staffed by two green-suited ladies who did little but sell pigeon seed all day. A gaggle of largely idle portrait photographers loitered around, as the usual armed array of police, soldiers and riot squad patrolled past.

From Arequipa, a jarring five-hour minibus ride over corrugated dirt tracks took me to Chivay at the gateway to Colca Canyon. At 3400m deep Colca is the world's second deepest canyon and is twice the depth of the Grand Canyon in Arizona. The giant fissure slices through the high Andes for over a hundred kilometres, creating epic scenery and a home for huge Andean condors.

We stopped at Mirador Cruz del Condor and watched the immense birds rise on thermals from between plunging canyon walls. Utilising their ten-foot wingspan and warm air to good effect they soared and circled effortlessly above us.

Condors are the biggest raptors on the planet and can weigh over 30 pounds. Feeding off carrion, they provide an important ecological clean-up role and coastal birds will even scavenge from whale carcasses washed ashore. The huge birds also had great spiritual significance to the Incas who believed they represented the highest plane of existence. They revered the sacred birds as messengers from the heavens and thought when someone died condor wings would carry them up to the afterlife.

ON THE RETURN journey, I fell violently ill and had to get our driver to pull off the road. By the time we reached Chivay, I was feverish, vomiting and feeling awful. The five-hour ride back to Arequipa was hell as my condition worsened forcing me frequently to stop the bus. Hopefully, the sight of me racing frantically for the scant cover of a small rock whilst fumbling to undo my trousers provided some amusement for the fellow passengers to distract them from all the delays!

Next morning I went to Arequipa's hospital to find an English-speaking doctor and discovered I had amoebic dysentery which could kill me if left untreated. It seemed likely that I'd picked up the deadly bug weeks earlier on the Inca trail as bouts of sickness and debilitating trots had plagued me ever since. Each time I had starved myself for a day in an attempt to cure it, drinking only foul tasting sugared, salted water to rehydrate. It worked for a while but now I knew why my symptoms kept coming back.

Starving myself was always difficult unless cuy picante was on the menu. This spicy-hot guinea pig dish is considered a Peruvian delicacy, but generally arrived on the plate looking like a rat had been run over and then pan-fried!

I left the hospital with a handful of pills, strict instructions on diet and a total ban on alcohol for a week. Bad timing as my birthday was four days away! But the Tambo Viejo hostel turned out to be the perfect place to rest and recuperate for a few days and watching tiny hummingbirds which frequented its garden helped while away the hours.

LEAVING AREQUIPA BEHIND I bused north towards Nasca over the Pan American Highway. The smooth tarmac of the world's longest road made a welcome change from the usual rib-rattling roads. The fast road hugged the coastline, and we swept past empty arid landscapes accompanied by pounding Pacific surf to our left. At almost 600 kilometres it was another long ride but provided more hours of enforced rest, and the scenery along the final stretch grew ever more spectacular with giant sand dunes and grand but strange rock formations.

Noisy roosters roused me early next day, which for once was fine as I had a flight to catch. Soon I was stepping into a tiny two-seater and taxiing down a baked dirt runway. Minutes later the single prop plane climbed to a few hundred feet, and the flat parched pampa below began to reveal strange geometric lines and shapes.

The Nasca Lines are thought to be 2000 years old and yet nobody knows for sure why they were drawn. Discovered in the thirties when commercial pilots first flew over the area, they have been the subject of study ever since.

Eight hundred lines have been etched into the dry desert floor along with 300 geometric figures and 70 animal and plant designs, called biomorphs. Several straight lines stretch for thirty miles, and the biomorphs grow from fifty to twelve hundred feet long.

We flew above a huge hummingbird, its white-winged outline contrasting with the dull rock of the desert. An abstract parrot came into view, then a condor, a curly-tailed monkey, a tree, a spider, strange hands and a vast trapezoid.

The arid landscape revealed more of the mysterious lines as our pilot flew on until the ground beneath us resembled a giant chalkboard. The region only receives twenty minutes of rainfall a year so the lines are well preserved, and it's been suggested they were made to please the Gods in the hope of being rewarded with more rain.

Other theories speculate that the lines represent an immense astronomical pre-Inca calendar, or perhaps tracks used in running contests, or even that the plain is a map of an ancient empire. One thing historians do seem to agree on is that they were formed by the Nasca people who flourished from AD 1 to 700.

From Nasca I journeyed on to Ica stopping en route to wander amongst an archaeological cemetery where centuries of wind had scoured sand from an ancient burial site, leaving behind a desert littered with human bones, skulls and macabre mummified remains.

In Ica I had a close call with thieves on a bus who stole from beneath our seat in broad daylight. During the journey I noticed my daypack had moved, so hooked it forwards, trapped it with my foot and thought no more about it. But when we reached a hostel BJ discovered cameras and belongings were missing from his bag.

Thinking back to the bus we remembered two guys had followed us aboard then forced the occupants from seats behind us. We felt their knees pushing into our backs but hadn't bothered turning around as it was normal on buses in South America. But now realisation dawned they had been diving under the seat and fishing inside our bags. Not a single passenger had said a word, and it seemed perhaps gringos were regarded as fair game.

Days later on a tour bus to Paracas I discovered the vast majority of its passengers had been robbed within the last week, one even at knifepoint whilst lying on a beach. Back in Cusco, a favourite trick of thieves had been chalk marking gringos using ATMs, following and then robbing them later. More worrying was a late-night tactic used on Colette who had a rope wrapped around her neck and came to lying in the road with her valuables missing.

TOWERING SEA ARCHES and rocky cliffs line the Paracas National Reserve coastline, whilst its islands are home to hundreds of thousands of seabirds and huge families of raucous sea lions. Birds blackened the skies as our boat sped towards the jagged outcrops and thousands of kamikaze-pilot-like petrels pierced the dark waters of the Pacific around us diving for dinner.

When our skipper nosed his small craft closer to the eroded islands, the cacophony erupting from the crowded colonies and stench of sea mammals assaulted our senses. Humboldt penguins peered down in curiosity at our passing as countless other species eyed us in wary alarm from white guano-stained perches. Motoring back towards the mainland a mini-squadron of pelicans skimmed the surface in perfect formation, then followed us ashore and squabbled over scraps fed from the boards of a jetty.

HEADING NORTH FROM Paracas to Pisco, I face-planted into the headrest when our bus was brought to a wild swerving emergency stop. We'd been doing about eighty on a smooth straight road when our driver stamped on the brakes, and as we slewed off the tarmac a commotion erupted as the door was hanging half detached. After futile attempts to fix it, the driver crow-barred it off completely, shoved it inside the luggage compartment and carried on. Within minutes we were back up to speed but now being blasted by cool air which had nowhere to go. For two hours we steadily froze as the driver seemed now in an even greater hurry to reach his destination!

THE NEXT LEG from Pisco to Lima was again north, and when we reached the capital's outskirts, it looked even more chaotic than La Paz. A noisy, nightmarish tangle of cabs, buses, bikes and trucks filled the dirty streets all competing for space. Vehicles bore battle scars worse than the doorless bus, and cars pushed past missing entire body panels. Many had neither bonnets nor headlights, and one truck lumbered by with its engine fully exposed!

On pothole-riddled pavements, street traders took every scrap of space, and the city was awash with armed police and military presence. Soldiers guarding the presidential palace kept passers-by on the move, and we weren't allowed to step on the pavement let alone stop.

Lima's centre was smart and clean, particularly

around the beautiful plaza surrounded by grand colonial architecture. I witnessed a wobbling Easter parade of two dozen men struggling under the weight of a huge statue of Jesus, borne for their sins on shoulders! Followed by 32 more staggering under a much bigger statue of Mary around the busy square.

Two days was long enough in the crowded, clamorous city. I caught up with friends and nosed around museums, but was soon heading for Huaraz and clean air of the mountains.

Nestled in a valley in the Cordillera Blanca, it's possible to see 23 snow-crested peaks over 5000 metres from the small town. When I arrived long hours after leaving Lima, all I wanted to see was a bed in a hostel, but the place proved tricky to find. I had an address, but struggled to locate the street and lost an hour lugging my laden pack around town. Nobody knew where it was, and in desperation I asked a policeman which can be an ill-advised thing to do in parts of Peru. Even he didn't know but phoned from the station, got directions, then offered to drop me there. At last he found the road and so I pulled up at my hostel in the back of a police car!

As I walked in and crossed the courtyard, I heard odd sounds and glanced up to the surreal sight of an Israeli squatting on the roof, backdropped by snow-capped peaks, playing a didgeridoo!

Cactus Juice at Charlie's

MANY TRAVELLERS BACKPACKING through South America follow a route known as the gringo trail, tracing the course of the Andes running north to south or vice versa. Throughout the continent, foreigners are known as gringos and with so many people visiting the same places, it was almost inevitable the route became known as this.

In southern Ecuador, Vilcabamba has become an essential stop on the trail for many, but at first glance there's little of note here, just a small settlement nestled between hills, built around a ubiquitous plaza. Guidebooks will tell you it's a great place to hike or relax, but what they probably won't mention is the cactus juice this sleepy spot is infamous for.

Also known as San Pedro, this local speciality is extracted from certain cacti species that grow on surrounding hillsides and yet the juice can't just be bought off the shelf in a bottle. The fact that it numbers amongst the planet's most powerful hallucinogens probably has much to do with this!

FOR FIVE MONTHS I'd followed the gringo trail north from Chile, to the Salar de Uyuni and Bolivia, before weaving my way through Peru and into Ecuador. Having spent many days hiking in Huaraz and around Cuzco, the hills of Vilcabamba held little appeal for more trekking. However, a lazy feet-up trip of a rather different nature sounded much more interesting…

NILS HAD DRAWN the short straw and been sent to Dr Pablo's dispensary to swap our dollars for doses of the magical local medicine, whilst the rest of us loitered anxiously by the plaza, unsure of the dubious transactions legality. But the deal was done without incident and soon we were headed towards Charlie's cabanas up in the hills, clutching little bags of cactus juice in the back of a pickup truck.

We checked in, chucked backpacks on bunks, then found the kitchen. Standing around a table, we contemplated our sagging collection of bags containing thick fibrous liquid. San Pedro is a nasty shade of green and it didn't look like something you would normally be tempted to drink. Knowing its reputation for having a foul taste we uncapped a dozen bottles of water and broke chocolate bars into bite-sized chunks.

We could only find a single cup to dispense the nefarious looking liquid, so had to the take it in turn. Nils knocked his back first, then handed me the cup. I tried to down it in one, but it proved impossible. It was disgusting. I necked the rest and crammed chocolate into my mouth to mask the vile taste, guzzling water, then stuffing more chocolate in. Retching followed the cup around the room as my friends forced down their doses.

The taste of cactus juice defies description but may be on a par with swigging petrol. The bodies reflex response is to eject it instantly. Just two mouthfuls were hard to swallow, more may have been impossible.

With plastic bags drained and chocolate wrappers empty we ambled down to an isolated cabana near a river. Surrounded by trees and lush hillsides it looked the perfect location, so with some chilled music playing, we lounged around awaiting the effects. Nothing happened for a while and nobody was seeing anything unusual, so I went for a wander.

I found myself in a field of tall corn, and as I pushed through sensed things were not quite normal around me. Colours seemed more vivid than usual and I felt incredibly attuned to my surroundings, totally at one with nature. My senses were heightened, my mind clear. I felt wide awake and very alive.

Leaving the field behind I took a narrow track and spotted a snake. I dislike snakes, so normally would have turned around and left, but instead I followed, transfixed by its form. As it slithered ahead, it seemed to leave a visible trail of movement and so appeared to be ever-growing in length. Realising my cactus juice was kicking in I retreated to the cabana.

The little group had now spread out, with people lounging on rocks by the river, or sitting immersed in its water. Two were perched up trees! I found myself a hammock and laid back to enjoy my private show.

Wherever I looked everything appeared to be growing. Suspended below an orange tree I stared in wonder as branches above me began to grow. Branches sprouted buds, buds became leaves, leaves grew larger. Fascinated by this high-speed nature, I watched oranges ripen until they started to rot. It was like viewing speeded-up time-lapse photography. Aware that I needed to maintain a positive mindset, I tore my eyes from the decay and watched the skies instead.

Music had blended with birdsong and the gurgling river and now cloud formations swirled and danced along in harmony. The intoxicating soundtrack and captivating hallucinations completely engulfed me.

Giant faces appeared in the sky with entrancing eyes that seemed to draw me up. Inca images and shapes from the Peruvian Nasca Lines, mixed perfectly with the faces and swirling formations above. As I gazed in rapt attention lines of little birds in diminishing size, flew past in undulating formation, flitting in and out of my vision.

Sometimes everything appeared as if looking through a semi-transparent fingerprint, other times it was like viewing through a microscope with red and blue blood cells moving and flowing over everything petri dish style.

Anywhere and everywhere I looked, everything was on the move. Grasses, leaves and plants were growing before my eyes. Meadows slid up and down hillsides. Black and white markings on cattle swapped between animals. Fields of sugarcane pushed forward in constant motion. Trees glided along hillcrests. Sections of surrounding fields separated in opposing directions.

All the while the music seemed to be building towards a massive crescendo as I lay beaming beneath mesmerising clouds spiralling higher and higher.

After many hours I rolled out of my hammock and somehow made it to the river; walking had become a whole new experience. I sat beside the flowing water watching rocks and stones grow then come to life as faces or patterns appeared in their grain. As the symphonic soundtrack continued to build, the river picked up pace, getting faster and faster, becoming almost frantic as it aligned with the music.

I wanted to explore and found a field of sugar cane, but the experience of entering its confines was too intense as I felt full of trepidation, mixed with wonder and nervous excitement. It was a sensory overload too much to take, and I could feel the ground drawing me.

Sprawling on a mat I became mesmerised by cigarette ashes burning down in a stream of chain-smoking. As the sun slipped from the sky incredible shadows stretched across hillsides, then as darkness descended hundreds of red, green and white fireflies danced around us in magical displays.

I fought the all too real sensation of being eaten alive by insects as I listened to Mica describe how she found herself at the top of a tree. She had no idea how she got there. Or how she got down again!

Later we made our way back to the hill cabana and found a campfire still burning. Gazing into the fire was like watching internal organs of a body working, sometimes grotesquely being consumed by worms or maggots. For two hours we sat transfixed by the burning embers.

With the fire dying we went to our beds. It was three am, and the sky was still alive with shapes, faces and symmetry, but when I neared my bunk, all I could see was coiled snakes.

I knew the serpents weren't there, but I could see dozens and had to force myself to grab a blanket, lie down and curl up. My cactus trip had lasted fourteen hours and when I closed my eyes, I could still see snakes. When the snakes faded away, I re-lived the rest of the incredible experience for as long as I could until I fell into a long weary sleep.

IN SOME PARTS of the world hallucinogenic plants have been used for centuries, maybe even millennia, during Shamanic rituals and ceremonies to access altered states of consciousness and attain spiritual enlightenment. In some cultures, they are still used for these purposes, and Shaman are important figures in these communities, revered as medicine men and healers.

By using these ancient and sacred visionary plants Shaman seek to help find balance and harmony on Earth and to develop, grow and perfect the soul.

AT AN EARLY point in evolutionary history, mankind made a huge leap forwards when hominids first became self-aware which science has been unable to explain. But there is growing evidence that the consumption of hallucinogenic mushrooms was instrumental in accelerating this leap to self-awareness with their mind-expanding properties.

In Terence McKenna's book Food of the Gods, he makes a strong case to support this idea and suggests that the widely growing mushrooms would have been found by foraging hunter-gatherers, and would have been consumed as food.

DRINKING A PLANT extract such as San Pedro, is just a way to access an alternative mind state, a way to unlock and experience a different level of consciousness. Perhaps it also taps into something ancient and fundamental, maybe trace memory of spiritual abilities we have lost because they are not encouraged in the modern world.

It's interesting that we live in a society where the mass use of highly addictive artificially produced prescription drugs is the norm, yet using a naturally occurring plant or fungi to explore altered states of consciousness is not just discouraged but criminalised.

In Canada and Peru, the hallucinogenic ayahuasca plant has been used to successfully treat harmful addictions to cocaine and heroin.

Who knows where further experimental research would lead…

La Selva. Coca, Ecuador

"STOP!"

"Don't move."

He came towards me brandishing a massive machete. I did as I was told and froze.

The long dark blade hovered inches from my neck.

Then, with a skilful flick of the wrist, it was over.

A small lurid green tree frog landed on the deck.

"Don't touch that. It's poisonous."

Moments earlier I'd felt something land on my shoulder as we forced our way through thick vegetation and luckily the guide stopped me before I had a chance to grab it. Glands secreted toxins onto the frog's skin, making it hazardous for humans to touch. Small enough to fit in the palm of my hand, its diminutive size belied the danger it posed. With the aid of his massive machete once more, Juan deftly flicked the frog back towards its domain.

Half-way into a six-day adventure down Rio Shiripuno, a small tributary of the mighty Amazon, we'd been exploring primary rainforest when the tree frog hopped aboard. Motoring for days to reach there in a twenty-foot long dug-out the rainforest had lived up to its name. It had poured relentlessly. During our second night, the river had risen by over two metres, and by day our canoe needed near-constant bailing under the endless deluge.

Despite the rain, the jungles steamy warmth was very welcome as just days earlier I'd been shivering in snow. Kitted out with crampons, twin ice axes and thermals a blizzard caught us on the 5000m summit of Tungurahua volcano, up above the village of Banos. The contrast could not have been more extreme.

To reach Coca, Ecuador's gateway to the Amazon, I'd taken one of the worst bus trips I had experienced in South America. Travelling through Bolivia, Peru and Ecuador, I had endured far too many long grim bus journeys totalling close to 300 hours in six months. Almost twelve whole days of my life!

Breakdowns, crashes, crazy drivers, even the door falling off in Peru. Aside from those inconveniences, most buses were dilapidated, overcrowded, hot and uncomfortable. Add treacherous potholed dirt tracks, mudslides, perilous inclines, river crossings, endless hairpin bends and you start to get the picture.

In Chile, buses and roads had been better but not much safer, and I soon learnt not to sit at the front. Time and again I saw windscreens with a crazed spiders web of fractured glass in the same place. The place where the front passenger's head had made violent contact, whipped forward by collisions…

But the gruelling overnight bus from Banos to Coca was worse than anything experienced before. Bus travel at night is never good, but journeying over atrocious dirt tracks on an overloaded vehicle with no suspension, no legroom and no seat padding was really no fun. The heat and humidity became ever more stifling as we descended from Banos into tropical lowlands of the Oriente. When we reached a crossing with a chain ferry, where our tired driver almost put us in the river, a dunk in cool water would have come as a welcome relief!

After ten long hours with little sleep, the ordeal ended as we arrived in Coca. The isolated oil town has a bad reputation, and on first impressions, it looked well deserved with ramshackle buildings, filthy streets and rough looking people. But for us, it was a fleeting visit, with just enough time for breakfast before meeting our guide. Soon we were aboard yet another bus, this time bound for the jungle.

After last night's stuffy journey, I needed fresh air and climbed on the roof along with an Aussie called Grant. With low-hanging branches and yet another would-be rally driver in the hot seat, it was an exciting ride as he tore along winding jungle roads with us clinging to the roof-rack. But it was far from comfortable and we quickly climbed down when a horrendous noise brought the bus to a premature halt.

The bumpy track had taken its toll, and the exhaust was broken. Half an hour later they had still failed to fix it, so just snapped it off and tossed it in the back! From then on a raucous unmuffled racket deafened us as we followed snaking lines of steaming oil pipes deeper into la selva.

For mile upon mile ten parallel pipes flowed around every bend; an impressive feat of engineering but an ugly, unwelcome intrusion into the unique environment. Fire-spouting refineries further scarred the landscape, each bulldozed from pristine rainforest. Despite driving for a considerable distance we never left the oil pipes behind.

AT LAST WE stopped at our pickup point and began loading supplies into a wooden dugout floating in the river below. Food crates, a heavy bunch of bananas and countless bottles of water were lobbed down the human chain. Finally, it took three people in the water to manhandle a huge fuel barrel on board as the canoe moved in the current. With the vital drum secured, we clambered aboard and set off on our six-day adventure.

Machete man Gordo sat in the bow, alongside our guide Juan Medina, with little Flaco at the helm. Later, we would pick up a grinning toothless guide from the local Huaorani tribe. Three Aussies and three Pommies made up the gringo contingent.

Leaving the track behind we motored downstream, making frequent forced stops to navigate over the tops of log jams and fallen trees. The thick brown water was a metre down from its normal level, but wouldn't stay that way for long.

Seated two by two down the length of our dugout, six pairs of tired eyes scanned dense banks as we headed for the interior. Despite feeling shattered from last night's endurance test, the anticipation of exotic species kept everyone on full alert as we had a chance of glimpsing an elusive jaguar or giant anaconda. Or, as Grant hoped, a jaguar eating an anaconda! But with anacondas in the area measuring up to nine metres, I wasn't so keen on a close encounter. That was longer than our dugout canoe!

A few hours later we stopped at a small collection of simple stilt huts, which were home to the Huaorani. It was a privilege to be shown around the tribe's primitive village, but it also felt intrusive as our cultures were so far apart. The more civilisation encroaches the less likely their traditional lifestyle will be maintained.

Crackling over an open fire was a blackened monkey, with others trapped in small cages awaiting similar fates. A hefty tapir foraged the cooking enclosure with piglets running underfoot, whilst a pair of colourful macaws peered down from nearby branches.

We met our toothless guide and discovered that missing molars were a common trait amongst the tribe. Juan thought it was probably due to poison-tipped blow-darts they still used for hunting. Toxin would still be in the kills system when they ate it, so would ingest traces which could accumulate over time. Waving farewell to the tribe, we pushed out into the flow and headed deeper into rainforest.

Despite intense scrutiny, by the time we reached camp only a handful of squirrel monkeys, parrots and toucans had been spotted, but it wasn't really surprising as we were still in secondary rainforest. Within minutes of beaching, undergrowth swallowed the crew as they hacked into it with machetes, re-emerging with freshly cut poles and bamboo stakes.

No time was wasted as tents and tarps were set up, and moments later the skies opened and the first of many instalments of heavy rainfall pummelled our shelters. Darkness falls fast in jungle, so after an open fire cooked dinner it was an early night enveloped by the exotic, relaxing sounds of la selva.

EARLY NEXT MORNING we struck camp, loaded the canoe and motored away. With oil exploration having an ever greater impact on the area, we aimed to get as far from Coca as we could, so planned to push on all day through the persistent rain.

Sharp eyes peered from beneath dripping ponchos, but we saw no sign of snakes. Black turtles comically back-flipped off logs at our approach and tiny kingfishers flashed past in a blur of colour. Raucous calls of Howler monkeys betrayed their presence high overhead in the canopy. Toucans and vibrant macaws glided above us, quickly disappearing again into greenery. Electric-blue butterflies larger than a hand danced by the dense river banks. Between heavy downpours, it was a rich, visual delight.

Sometimes Flaco would nose us into a side stream, squeezing through the smallest of gaps, as Gordo on the prow hacked through the undergrowth, spraying us with foliage, huge insects, spiders and the poisonous frog.

Once through, we emerged into dark mysterious pools dappled with light. Sometimes we'd stop to fish for piranha, using chunks of meat to catch the tasty plate-sized dinner. Other times we would push on exploring further, ever eager to spot more wildlife.

Every detour we made and every bend we rounded became a voyage of discovery and a fresh chance for a new encounter. The deeper we probed the greater the sense of adventure, especially when we reached primary rainforest. An environment so wild and untouched it seemed impossible anyone had been there before.

AT NIGHT WE slipped out in the dugout and sliced through inky eerie waters in search of alligators. With the aid of torches, we scanned for telltale pairs of red predator eyes. When a gator was spotted, Juan signalled the boys into action, stealthily paddling the canoe closer. With torches blinding our prey, we eased through bushes towards its lair. Often, a lightning-fast blur and a big splash was our only reward. But when we got close enough, Juan launched himself at the gator, grabbing it then lifting it in amongst cheering gringos.

We passed our toothy trophy around for photos, gripping its armoured neck and tail tightly. A three-foot prehistoric reptile loose in our dugout in the dark didn't bear thinking about.

NIGHTS AND DAYS blended together in a wonderful cycle of adventure. Patrolling the riverbanks, making or breaking camp, swimming, jungle hikes, gator hunting, fishing, fire building. And bailing!

Aside from hearing the Howler's roars we spotted many more species of monkey and were privileged to see three rare giant otters at close range. Screeching in alarm they appeared from nowhere, came straight at us, dove under the dugout then disappeared again. With impenetrable jungle on both sides, no doubt we were seen by many more animals than we spotted, but exotic birds flitted past as we scanned the banks for rarer sights.

On our last day, as the final hours of the expedition slipped away, so did our hopes of glimpsing a jaguar, or even an anaconda. With ever decreasing habitat, jaguar numbers are in decline and sightings rare, but normally anaconda can be seen sunning themselves on the riverbanks. Due to the never-ending rain, our luck was out and not one put in even a brief appearance.

The closer we came to so-called civilisation, the more evidence we saw of man's negative impact on the rainforest. For us, it was another reminder of our reluctant return to reality, but for the region, a sad sign of the times. More examples of the destruction and environmental disaster that's happening all around the Amazon at an alarming pace.

LOSING GLOBALLY IMPORTANT, irreplaceable rainforest, a unique habitat containing undiscovered species and endless biodiversity, in the pursuit of profit is plain madness and has to stop.

Our planet's reserves have been plundered for far too

long with scant regard for consequence. It took millenia for the world to evolve into equilibrium and yet mankind has destroyed so much in less than a century.

Earth is our home. It sustains us.

Isn't it time we started to look after it?

The responsibility is everyones.

Hawaii
1998

Aloha Maui

SIX MONTHS IN South America had left me with little money, no credit card and no onward ticket. Flights to the UK were expensive, and I had neither job nor home to return to. I did, however, have family in California, but even flying there from Quito was costly. Having never visited North America it seemed opportune and thought that if I could get to L.A. I could stay with my uncle, find some casual work and see something of the country. So I settled on the cheapest option and spent almost all my remaining funds on a flight to Florida and hoped I could work out the next leg when I landed!

Before I even entered the States, immigration stopped me in my tracks. An officious border guard didn't like an answer I gave and pressed a buzzer. Moments later I was taken to a room full of darker-skinned faces than mine and told to sit. And no, I could not make a phone call. Sit down, shut up and wait.

The problem was I had no onward ticket, which was a condition of visa waiver entry, but I couldn't afford a flight to L.A. let alone another one home, so knew that I'd have to wing it on arrival.

After a lengthy, anxious wait, my name was called and this time I was led into a small cell-like room.

Fortunately, my interrogator believed a wildly exaggerated figure of available funds and warmed to my partially fabricated story about a film producer uncle, living near Hollywood who I would stay with. This was close to the truth, so it was easy to be convincing, but also the prospect of being turned away and flown back to South America was motivating to say the least!

AFTER ECUADOR, MIAMI seemed false, unfriendly and far too expensive. For two days I explored by bike whilst searching for lifts or rental car returns, but found nothing so settled on a bus ticket instead. One hundred and twenty bucks sounded like a bargain, and after enduring so many buses in South America thought three days aboard a bus over better roads wouldn't be too bad. I was wrong.

The bus had no headrests, and neither did it have a radio, let alone a video player. Even buses in South America had those. Often along with a small drinks cabinet for the driver too!

Oh well, I was only aboard for the next three thousand miles…

HAVING HOPED TO have driven across the country myself, I was looking forward to seeing the States. But it didn't take long to be glad I hadn't, as aside from endless flat multi-lane freeways arrowing ahead, after we left Florida there was little to see. Well, apart from the sprawling multicoloured fast-food chain stretching steadily west.

BellMcBurgersWingHut, PapaKingDonaldsDriveIn, DunkinDennysdrearyDiner, WendyJacksFatnFries-Franchise…

Within hours I hardly bothered to glance up from my book, and when I did the landscape was unchanged, aside from maybe the name on a neon sign above the cholesterol store. Soon it became a dreary cycle of dozing, bum-cheek positioning and page turning, punctuated by stops for food and fuel. Groundhog day aboard a Greyhound bus!

All too slowly my bus swallowed up miles along the busy concrete highways, eventually crossing eight states and going through four time zones. After sixty-two hours with little visual stimulation aside from Mississippi's long, low-slung bridges, a spectacular sunset over Houston, and a multicoloured blob in the middle of nowhere aptly named The Thing, I arrived in L.A.

My journey had been an endurance test of discomfort, sleep deprivation and a dreary battle with boredom. Several times I changed buses, but always in the middle of the night, just when I'd fallen asleep.

At the outset, I noticed my itinerary read: Greyhound Lines Inc. Not good for travel. They were certainly right about that!

FLICKING THROUGH THE L.A. Times one morning I spotted some bargain flights to Maui and decided I had to go. But I was flat broke, and with no work permit had little chance of earning much Stateside. There was only one option, so reluctantly I returned home.

Back in the UK, I landed a dull job where I worked every hour possible and saved every penny. Six months later I boarded another jet back to L.A. Two weeks on, and I was taxiing onto the tarmac at LAX once more…

AS THE AIRCRAFT made its final approach over a beautiful blue expanse of Pacific, I got my first glimpse of the island with its lush rugged mountains fringed with golden beaches and white surf. Mark Twain described Hawaii as 'the loveliest fleet of islands that lies anchored in any ocean' and from the air it looked like he was right.

Hawaiian warmth welcomed me as I stepped onto concrete at Kahului and gazed across the runway to palms and huge pounding surf beyond. Outside the airport, I stuck out my thumb and soon afterwards booked into Banana Bungalows in Wailuku. Within the week I'd hired windsurfing kit and a car for the duration and checked into the termite suite at Jerome's. But I'd also spent three-quarters of my funds. Food and even beer would now have to be rationed for the next seven weeks!

JEROME'S SURF SHACK in Piai stood in an idyllic spot just back from a beach, but the place was falling down, helped along by hungry termites. At night I could hear them munching the wooden wall behind my head! Being in a prime location on the north shore, his land was worth a lot, so Jerome seemed content to let the critters keep chewing until the old place collapsed. In the meantime, he let out rooms to the likes of me, surfers and windsurfers chasing their dreams with little money.

My rental car was known as a Maui cruiser; a battered, budget, rusting piece of junk with questionable legality. Naturally, the hire shop assured me it was fully road legal, and I hoped they were right because its exhaust pipe had so many holes, police would hear me from miles away. The ageing Mazda came equipped with a bent wooden stick, just the right size to help prop the hatchback open!

HAWAII, AND IN particular Maui, is home to many windsurfing legends and world champions, due to the consistent winds and waves the islands are blessed with. In fact, Maui boasts some of the best conditions found anywhere on the planet. Add to that warm year-round ocean temperatures, and you have a mecca for surfers and windsurfers alike.

Surfing started hundreds of years ago in Polynesia and was first witnessed by Europeans in 1778 when Captain Cook's ships explored the region. In the early twentieth century, the sport spread around the world, initially, to places like Australia and California, where surf culture is still huge, but Hawaii remains the spiritual home of surfing.

Windsurfing, by comparison, is a new sport which only took off in the seventies. The first world championship was held in 74, and ten years later it was adopted into the Olympics at the L.A. games. Once again the sport was led by Hawaiians, being a nation of watermen and because of the island chain's ideal conditions.

By the eighties, the sport was growing fast and had gained a huge worldwide following. With more competitions came ever-growing media coverage attracting big-name sponsorship. It was the start of an era when newly crowned stars of windsurfing became household names. People like the now legendary Robby Naish who won his first world championship aged just thirteen, then went on to win the title twenty-three more times. A Hawaiian…

Windsurfing today isn't as popular as it was at its peak in the eighties, but it's still practised by tens of thousands of people around the planet. The fast, exciting, adrenaline sport is highly addictive and always challenging due to the ever-changing nature of wind and water. There's little to match the feeling of blasting flat out across the ocean on a fast, responsive board, jumping off ramps and carving turns, as you harness the raw energy of wind in your sail.

TERMITES HAD BEEN chewing the wall again and were in danger of starting a secondary infestation inside my brain. Hearing insects eating wall inches from your head whilst lying semi-awake in the silent small hours for some reason does strange things to dreams! Sunlight put a stop to the nocturnal visions, so I got up, pulled on my board shorts, slung a surfboard under one arm, and padded barefoot along the high street. Turning right a sandy footpath led me through palms down to the shoreline. I waded into warm shallow water, jumped on my board and paddled out to the break. Sitting in the lineup, I looked back ashore. Behind the beach and postcard perfect palms, a lush tropical landscape stretched inland, climbing towards the towering slopes of Haleakala volcano. The sun was out, the swell was up, I couldn't imagine a better start to my day. For this, I could put up with termites any time!

WHILST AWAITING THE arrival of trade winds I explored the island, setting out to drive the fabled Hana Highway, along with two fellow windsurfers from Jerome's. Billed as one of the world's most spectacular drives, this amazing coastal road winds around the eastern end of the island.

For fifty miles the snaking route hugs cliffs above black lava and pounding surf, or plunges into dark valleys dripping with vegetation. There are almost 600 tortuous bends and over 50 single lane bridges, mostly alongside waterfalls. And in many places, the twisting road isn't wide enough for two cars to pass.

Sometimes we drove through lush rainforest or dense mysterious groves of towering bamboo, other times travelling along cliffs high above volcanic beaches of red and black sands. We stopped to explore blowholes, caves and pools, then at Waianapanapa park, to watch massive surf smashing into lava lining its bay, showering spray fifty feet in the air.

With constant bends, it was fun to attack even in my tired old cruiser, and as tourists are encouraged to move over for locals, most drivers got out of our way as the Mazda definitely didn't look or sound like a hire car!

By the time we set off towards Paia it was dusk, so gambled on a shortcut back. Tarmac soon degenerated into bumpy dirt track, bringing an opportunity to test the cars rally credentials. But with single candlepower headlights and an occasional suicidal cow standing in the road, it turned into another exciting drive!

ANOTHER OF MAUI'S incredible roads leads up Haleakala; the world's largest dormant volcano, measuring a colossal seven-and-a-half miles long by two-and-a-half wide. The road from coast to summit is 37 miles long and runs in a relentless chain of switchback hairpin bends. For a fat fee, you can take a minibus tour arriving on top in time for sunrise, before being handed a bike to freewheel back down again.

I soon discovered these trips were expensive, but also conducted at a sedate, controlled pace on the roll down, with riders cocooned in safety protection. So having a hire car and looking for more adrenaline I came up with an alternative adventure.

Leaving the hostel before dawn, I drove inland and started my noisy ascent up the winding crater road, reaching the summit an hour or so later. Joining a small crowd, I sat beneath fading stars watching rugged silhouetted ridges emerge under the lightening skies. As dawn's muted colours replaced darkness, more of the massive volcano was revealed. Below, a huge bank of cloud encircled the summit, enshrouding the island.

As the sun crept higher, the crater's impressive expanse was illuminated, revealing dramatic shadows and unusual colours. I sat watching the captivating spectacle, waiting for the clouds and people to disperse, before setting off alone down Sliding Sands Trail into the crater.

Haleakala, which means House of the Sun in the Hawaiian language, has been dormant for 200 years, but it's still a very desolate place. Despite the name, it resembles a moonscape and was used to train astronauts before moon landings. A wide palette of browns, orange, yellows, reds and black paint the spartan lunar landscape. Clumps of spiky silverside plants sprout sporadically amongst rock and lava, adding patches of green and silver to the strange alien scenery.

The scale of the crater is immense, and after two hours of constant descent, I'd only made it a quarter of the way down. Far below, in the bowels of the volcano, a dozen or more cinder cones dotted the crater floor.

Under bright blue skies and blazing sun, I hiked deeper with barely a soul in sight, enhancing the sensation of being on another planet. After five hours of descent, the trail turned and led to a spectacular winding track etched into the crater wall. An hours climb later I reached tarmac once more, leaving me the prospect of a long hot hike up to the top. Luckily, I hitched a lift and soon found myself back on the summit.

KNOWING THE CYCLISTS would now be off the road, I thought I should have a clear run down the volcano. I turned the key, drove to the top of the slope, slid my rusty Mazda into neutral and started rolling. My challenge was to reach the bottom without putting the car in gear!

On steep smooth tarmac the car soon gained speed, so before long I was bowling along accompanied by sounds of squealing tyres. Countless fast, banked, bends sweeping back and forth down the slope made the road a drivers dream. Perfect visibility meant I could pick my lines and carry speed, reaching over sixty on straights, and the empty road made it easy to coast past the handful of cars I caught.

For eleven miles, I freewheeled as fast as possible down the massive volcano, torturing the tyres and stretching my cheeks as my grin grew wider. Much more fun than gliding sedately down on a bike, wrapped up in body armour!

IN WINTER, THE Hawaiian archipelago is visited by large numbers of humpback whales, who use the safety of warm shallow waters to raise their calves. It's estimated more than half of the entire North Pacific's population, believed to be around two thousand, visit the islands, travelling 3000 miles from the frigid waters of Alaska.

With so many huge mammals in the water, it's common to see whales from the shore. Often they breach, launching forty-tonne bulks out of the water, sometimes at the same moment as their calves. A truly spectacular sight.

By law, you have to stay a certain distance from them, but that can be difficult when you're windsurfing and one surfaces nearby. And when a fifty-foot leviathan launches itself skywards close by, worrying about breaking a law is the last thing on your mind!

WINDSURFING FROM THE wide scenic bay of Kahului is epic beneath the imposing bulk of West Maui Mountains. Both whales and sharks lurk in its blue waters. Overhead, jetliners come in low to land, whilst helicopters buzz above the breaking waves. Launching from warm, wind-rippled shallows you accelerate towards the surf line. Hitting a perfectly formed ramp at speed rockets the board skywards, right over the reef break. Hanging airborne for seconds, then landing hard and charging flat out for the horizon. Finally, gybing around on a heavy wall of swell you come tearing back in, flying along, fully powered up. Catching a wave and carving lines, you blast back at the golden beach, before cranking a wide flowing turn then heading out for more.

With an ever-changing liquid terrain and a well powered up sail, the board clatters along, throwing up salty spray and leaving a ragged white wake. As the small fin struggles to maintain grip in the water, the rider flirts with the risk of a wipeout. One moment he is blasting flat out over the water, the next, spat violently into it.

Hurled headfirst like a helpless rag doll. Moments later after a swim, a few shakes of the head to clear orifices, a quick waterstart back onto the board and the windsurfer is again speeding across the surface, seeking out his next ramp…

FURTHER EAST IS Hookipa beach park, one of Maui's most famous spots. With winters regular twenty-foot plus swell rolling in, Hookipa becomes a playground for pros or a place to sit amongst spectators taking in the free show. Watching local sailors tearing up powerful waves, launching huge aerials and landing double loops from ridiculous heights.

Along from Hookipa is another legendary spot where a monstrous wave known as Peahi, or Jaws breaks. In winter months, when it's working, this massive wave reaches heights of over sixty feet, and has been surfed and windsurfed when it's that size!

Standing on nearby cliffs watching this awesome force of nature is spellbinding. Dark, parallel, swell lines stretch towards the horizon, dividing up a whitecap speckled expanse of North Pacific. Half a mile offshore an underwater shelf ramps up swell into towering walls of water, moving at 25 mph. As each enormous wave breaks, colossal avalanches of foaming white water crash down, throwing up heavy spray and a thunderous roar.

When a surfer or windsurfer catches a wave, its true scale is revealed as the rider is dwarfed by a liquid mountain bearing down on him. Only the world's best watermen dare brave this behemoth.

The ride and rush must be electrifying, but mistakes here are heavily punished. Held underwater in the violence of the rinse cycle, surfers become disorientated as they are spun like rag dolls in the turmoil. Jet ski safety crews are on hand to fish out fallers, but even they are taking on a risky role, as there may only be a twenty-second rescue window before the next monster wave breaks. Nazaré in Portugal is the only place in the world where bigger waves have been ridden. Waves there have been surfed to over eighty feet!

MY RETURN TICKET was from Oahu, so after seven weeks on Maui, I reluctantly left the island paradise behind and flew to Hilo on the island of Hawaii. The Big Island, as it's known, is home to two of the worlds most active volcanoes, Kilauea and Mauna Loa. Mount Kilauea has been erupting continuously since 1983, and the resulting lava flows have covered over 100 square kilometres of land. It's also destroyed 200 homes and added many acres of land-mass to the island.

At 32,000 ft, Mauna Loa is higher than Mt Everest when measured from its seafloor base. The entire Hawaiian chain was formed by volcanism over seventy million years ago and still they continue to grow. A new island is forming under the ocean as the Pacific plate pushes the islands off a hotspot deep below in Earth's mantle.

IN CONTRAST TO my Haleakala hike, the weather on

Kilauea's summit was more in keeping with the bleak surroundings. Standing exposed on the rim of the massive caldera, a blustery wind swirled around as cool rain spattered down. Hundreds of feet below, huge cracks zigzagged across the black crust, and vents spewed white plumes of steam from a molten lava pool below. Dotted around the rim lay fresh offerings of fruit and flowers to Pele, the volcano goddess, adding spots of colour to the desolate and largely monochrome landscape.

It's a primordial place, and I sensed the power of the slumbering giant smouldering beneath my feet. It didn't feel like a place to linger, and I wasn't surprised islanders left gifts to appease Pele.

Driving down Crater Rim road we entered rainforest of giant tree ferns and ohia, then stopped to hike to Thurston Lava Tube. Surrounded by birdsong and dripping foliage we clambered down into a dark chamber almost big enough to drive a train through. The rough tunnel was formed when the outer crust of a river of molten lava cooled and hardened as its liquid core continued to flow. Centuries of eruptions have created a hidden labyrinth of lava tunnels on Hawaii, and according to our guide, one tube on the island stretched for forty miles.

The dank subterranean cavern was an eerie place to explore and felt likely to be inhabited by crawling otherworldly species and nefarious spiders, so I was glad to escape and breathe fresh air again.

With daylight fading, we made a final stop at the End of The Road, which, literally, it was. In front of our minibus, line markings on tarmac disappeared under smooth black lava which had flowed across at right angles, engulfing the road completely before continuing down to the coast. No barriers or detours stood, just a simple sign warning that hiking to the lava flow was dangerous. One mile away over a crusty barren landscape, massive white steam clouds belched from the ocean where red-hot molten lava poured from land into sea.

For an hour, we stumbled across the lava field, aided slightly by the feeble torches provided. It was tough terrain to navigate with giant cracks and collapsed lava tubes to negotiate. As darkness devoured steam, an orange glow appeared in the gloom, revealing the lava-flow.

The nearer we got the more unnerving it became underfoot, as it was easy to imagine liquid lava running underneath the crust. Beneath my boots, shiny rope-like formations of lava looked fresh, and less than a hundred feet away was a bubbling, spitting stream of molten lava.

Unlike more typically explosive continental volcanoes, Hawaiian ones produce fiery fountains and rivers of molten lava. Here, the lava stream was creeping towards the sea, and sporadically, a great glob of red-hot lava rolled forward engulfed in a ball of fire, pouring out smoky gases.

Despite the lava's slow pace and its distance from us, it was another place instinct told me not to linger.

THE FOLLOWING DAY a three-hour bus ride took me to Kona, where I just managed to jump aboard the last dive boat leaving its dock. With the sun sinking into a liquid horizon, we motored from port accompanied by a huge pod of spinner dolphin, showing off in the boat's wake. Following rocky coastline to Kona Surf Resort, we anchored close to a pair of boats probing the depths with powerful dive lights.

The sky was dark as I donned wetsuit and tank before stepping apprehensively off the stern. This was only my third ever night dive, and Jaws music playing in my head had accompanied the last! I signalled okay to the skipper, purged my BCD then sunk into the depths. Several divers were kneeling on the bottom with torches, giving an easy target to aim for, but maintaining station in the current was another matter. For minutes I battled with my buoyancy and an urge to bolt for the surface.

My twin torches soon attracted thick clouds of plankton, but they greatly reduced visibility, which was unnerving underwater at night. Wearing only a thin hired wetsuit, I was getting cold and being buffeted by strong current as I struggled to peer through plankton soup.

Suddenly a huge, ghost-like form emerged from the gloom and glided towards me. Its gaping mouth came straight at my face, so I could see right down the cavernous throat. I forgot to breathe as I stared wide-eyed at the monstrous mouth heading for me. Then at the last moment it turned and skimmed over my head, grazing my mask as it passed. It was only then I remembered the dive-master told me to hold on to my facemask, and not to forget to breathe!

The massive Manta ray disappeared before swooping around for a second helping of plankton soup. Again it came straight at me, with its three-foot wide mouth aimed right at my head, but yet again at the last moment swerved up over me. With my lights continuing to attract masses of plankton, the Manta made repeated passes, gorging itself on its prey. Its graceful wings made it appear to be flying with perfect precision as it swept past just centimetres away.

As the ghostly ten-foot wide shape materialized from the inky waters and swerved amongst us, it felt like a massive, marauding sea monster was in our midst. The so-called Devil Ray was living up to its name!

Manta rays have cephalic fins to funnel seawater into their mouths and use gill rakers to filter out tiny organisms, and it didn't take long for it to mop up the plankton. As the huge ray melted away into darkness, I made a slow ascent to the surface and was soon climbing a dive ladder out of the ocean.

Back aboard I cracked open a beer to celebrate what had turned out to be an exceptional birthday!

THE FOLLOWING DAY I flew to Oahu, and two days later returned to L.A.

One week later I landed back in the UK.

It was snowing!

Grand Cayman 2000

Swimming with Stingrays

FOUR HUNDRED KILOMETRES south of Cuba, in the middle of the Caribbean Sea, lies a cluster of small islands. Barely noticeable on a world map the Cayman Islands comprise Little Cayman, Grand Cayman and Cayman Brac. The islands are probably best known for their status as an offshore tax haven, and according to the book and movie world, stories abound of tax evasion, money laundering and hidden illicit fortunes.

Grand Cayman is in fact home to over 600 banks, most of which are miraculously squeezed into one modest building, and at which there only ever appears to be a single person working. The giant, menacing security guard!

However, aside from all the rumours regarding money, there is much more to the idyllic tropical islands.

GRAND CAYMAN IS visited by tens of thousands of tourists each year, many of whom stopover for less than a day, having arrived aboard cruise ships. Disembarking in Georgetown they flock to gift shops or head for the sandy expanse of Seven-mile beach.

All the islands are blessed with spectacular diving in the rich warm waters that surround them, and they support a thriving dive industry. The Cayman trench plunges to 25,000 feet, so scuba divers can certainly expect the unexpected!

Aside from superb diving, stunning beaches and the duty-free shopping for visiting cruise shippers, Stingray City is Grand Cayman's number one tourist attraction.

DESPITE BEING THE largest in the group, Grand Cayman is only twenty-two miles long and has a large bite missing from its top end, creating an eight-mile-wide u-shaped bay known as the North Sound. A barrier reef stretches across the mouth of the bay protecting the island, and midway a small gap in the coral has resulted in a shallow sandbar forming inside, making a perfect spot for returning fisherman to gut the morning's catch in safety.

Nature always exploits opportunity and stingrays soon gathered at the sandbar to mop up free offerings thrown overboard. Some years later this phenomenon was noticed by two maverick divers who then started to hand feed the rays. Businesses began to exploit the opportunity as well, and tourist boats arrived bearing fare-paying passengers.

MY OFFICE DESK sat on an uneven carpet of fine white sand, with a warm onshore breeze bringing the air conditioning. Above, a rustling palm frond canopy provided some much-needed shade and a restful soundtrack. Views from beneath the trees were sublime, with calm, crystal-clear, turquoise water stretching to meet deeper, darker water leading to the horizon. Waverunners bumping at mooring and a solitary speed boat tied to the long jetty were the only signs of humans. Behind me on warm sand stood a selection of beach toys, a bar, the dive shop and one tiny gift store. Not much.

Rum Point, named after barrels of rum got washed ashore from a shipwreck, was relatively underdeveloped due to its remote location from the capital Georgetown. Aside from Red Sail Sports small complex, there was little more than a hotel and several large, expensive, but often empty properties. Idyllic.

CORAL QUEEN, A glass-bottomed snorkelling boat, was generally skippered by local Caymanian legend Jimmy Ebanks, well, providing he was sober that day! Based at Rum Point the red boat was the closest to Stingray City and one of the first to take tourists to the sandbar. Jimmy was a colourful character, with a wealth of knowledge and experience of the waters, but like many islanders, had a weakness for the rum.

As watersports instructor, part of my job entailed crewing aboard Coral Queen, which over time became something of a love-hate experience. But at first, I felt full of trepidation.

MOTORING FOUR MILES offshore the sea lightens to an entrancing shade of pale turquoise as our boat glides over the sandbar. The sound of an approaching engine and steel hull attracts rays, drawing them in from deeper surrounding water. Over the years they have become conditioned like Pavlov's dogs. As I drop anchor Coral

Queen becomes surrounded by two dozen large, dark shapes. Called Stingrays. And I have to get in the water with them!

Having already chopped some squid, I have no excuses for further delay so lower steps from both sides of the stern. Jimmy is giving his slow speech full of corny jokes as I climb down the ladder and jump off, waiting first for a large space between the gathering rays. Immediately several dark shapes glide towards me and instinct tells me to move away, but I'm restricted by the weight of water. Their environment.

They brush past my legs, feeling surprisingly soft and smooth and I start to relax. But only a little as each has a ten-inch-long stinging barb above their tails.

The big black shapes encircling our boat have made the tourists less eager to enter the water and I'm unsure whether Jimmy's ramblings have helped. Slowly they descend the steps and come to me for squid and reassurance. I give them squid.

My next task is to catch one! I am not convinced that I should, but it's my job, so I have to try.

I hold a piece of squid at full arm's length and reluctantly bring it towards me, but the ray simply sucks in the squid and clears off. Second attempt, same result. I crouch lower and try again, this time another stingray gets a free snack and slides over my shoulder.

Jimmy, laughing, calls me over, Big Mary is cuddled in his arms. Not a tourist from Florida, but his favourite ray, a huge dark beast measuring four foot across. He shows me how it's done, with Mary perfectly playing her part.

Getting as low in the water as possible I target a much smaller ray and hold out some squid. Drawing it towards me, I let go of the snack just as the ray sucks, and extend both arms to guide the ray to my chest. With the stingray's snout in my sternum and my arms supporting it, I just have to move with the ray to keep it there. Simple! But I'm still nervous about its large stinging barb that's now rather too close to my face. Judging by the reactions and squeals around me I'm not alone in feeling slightly uncomfortable.

TIME SPENT IN the water watching and working with rays, and benefitting from Jimmy's wealth of experience, gradually gave me confidence to experiment with the stingrays. Being first into the water meant time alone with rays and my favourite trick necessitated wearing a weight belt and dive mask. Holding my breath and laying flat on my back on the sand, I could feed rays as they cruised a foot above my face. Free-diving then finning alongside them was an amazing experience, especially when they wore a bar jack backpack; a reef fish that likes to accompany rays swimming inches above their heads in hope of easy food.

Usually, the rays were passive, and even grabbing a tail resulted only in a squirm as they tried to escape. In eighteen months on the island, I never heard of a single person being stung. Steve Irwin, the famous Australian wildlife expert killed by a stingray off Queensland's Great Barrier Reef, was probably pushing his luck with a ray not conditioned to people, and it ran out when the ray responded with its only defence mechanism. If the barb hadn't penetrated his heart, he would still be with us. And still pushing his luck no doubt…

AS MORE TOURIST operators ran trips to the sandbar, and more free squid was on offer, so more opportunistic feeders arrived. Aside from fast-moving bar jacks, needle-nose fish would often steal the squid. Lightning fast and almost invisible from above, their sword-like snouts are lined with razor-sharp teeth, resulting in shredded fingers several times for me. Birds too could be a menace trying to grab squid, and once I heard a rumour of a rogue shark patrolling the sandbar.

BEING IN HURRICANE alley, sometimes the islands got pounded by heavy weather. Strong winds meant rough seas; not tourist friendly for people standing waist deep in water. So trips got cancelled, boats didn't visit the sandbar, and the stingrays didn't get fed. The resident group of rays was reckoned to comprise around eighty individuals, which came and went, but some rays had become lazy and totally conditioned, relying on tourists for easy food.

When the weather improved Coral Queen would be the first boat back to the sandbar. But if more than a few days had passed, the stingrays would be starving and their usual cat-like, rubbing around ankles behaviour would change to one of aggression in their quest for food.

Conch is a favourite food for rays that fend for themselves and conch, like most shellfish, are strongly attached to their homes, the shell. The suck of a stingray is so powerful it can pull a conch out of its shell, so when a hungry, aggressive ray sucks your back or thigh it can be painful. And excruciating in more sensitive areas as one unlucky male dive instructor discovered!

Stingrays mouths don't contain teeth, instead, they have two bony plates for crushing food, which is a fortunate as a greedy one tried to swallow my squid flavoured hand. On another occasion, a more optimistic one got most of my foot in its mouth as I dove for the bottom. Generally, though the stingrays were a real pleasure to be around, you simply had to ensure you weren't crewing aboard Coral Queen after a spell of bad weather!

MONTHS LATER ON the other side of the island, I was cruising back to Cayman Windsurf on our snorkel boat when I noticed a large dark shape moving rapidly down the reef. It was too fast for a stingray or spotted eagle ray, so thinking it must be a shark I steered towards it. As we got closer my suspicion was confirmed as it swerved away from the reef and came streaking towards us. It was chasing down a sizeable barracuda which torpedoed straight at us then disappeared under the boat.

At the last second, the shark noticed our hull and

slewed violently sideways to a stop. Its back and dorsal fin slashed out of the water and its broad head was only metres from our bow. The hammerhead seemed confused and at first stayed floating on the surface before slowly swimming away.

For several minutes we followed the magnificent eight footer through crystal clear shallows until it melted into the cover of reef once more.

It had been the barracuda's lucky day, as well as ours!

Nurse sharks could often be spotted resting under the protection of coral heads, and at a Breakers restaurant lemon sharks were fed fish scraps from the shore, but the hammerhead was a rare visitor to the islands.

Barracuda, however, were common and the warm waters were full of them, and I heard the wooden jetty at Rum Point was home to a large one. Using the cover of its piles, I stealthily finned towards the end and got within touching distance of the long toothy missile, which shot away at the last moment. Then suddenly it turned and speared at my face, swerving off again at the last second. With silver flanks displaying prominent black stripes, a clear sign of aggression, it flashed back and forth trying to drive me away. The long underslung jaw was hanging agape exposing rows of savage looking teeth, so I soon vacated his lair and swam out into open water!

A RADIO CALL from Captain Ron alerted me to a big shoal of baitfish being stalked by a massive barracuda, so

I steered a course towards his boat and dropped anchor. From the surface, I could see a circling ball of fish stretching thirty feet across, and lurking below was the dark shape of the 'cuda. I waited until the big predator was on the far side of the baitfish, took a deep breath then dived for the bottom.

As I swam into the shoal, the fish just parted around me and continued on their path, so I became encircled by thousands of silverfish. It was impossible to see more than a foot in front of my mask as I finned through the dense shoal until the last of them parted leaving me face to face with the gaping jaws and dead-eyed stare of a monstrous five-foot barracuda.

The massive predator was only feet away, but with a huge ball of prey herded up, it had no interest in me, and with a flick of its tail carried on circling as I swam for the surface and some much-needed air.

On both occasions, I'd pushed my luck with big barracuda, so when I noticed three large shapes shadowing me as I explored a coral garden labyrinth, I decided this time to retreat to the boat. Snorkelling a remote reef I felt unnerved by their size and presence as they continued to circle me. Knowing barracuda rarely attack swimmers was one thing. But being alone in their domain, constrained by spiky stag coral and shallow water, sensing I was being stalked by three massive ones was quite another matter!

Popeye Hitler and the Surf Shack

A STICKER ON the back of the Rolls Royce said Caveman Windsurf, the second one read Turtlehead Divers.

The Rolls was parked outside its owner's club. A modest affair. Just like his car.

The club was, in fact, a complex of luxury apartments surrounding a pool, built on white sand beach. Prime real estate really.

The pool had probably been put in for Americans, who seemed to really like his swanky resort. But who seemed somewhat confused by the sea. The sea that surrounds the small island.

Where do those little byrds live?

Oh, you mean the flying fish? Yes, those little byrds…

Is there an ATM at Stingray City?

No, ma'am, there isn't, it's where the stingrays live. In the sea.

Can I git three emptey bauwtles?

Why, ma'am? I wanna collect saamples of the different colours of sea wauter…

Yanks. Whaddya gonna do!

NEXT TO THE imposing glamour of Morris's Fortuna Club, a small tumbledown shack was tucked away off to one side. Almost hidden. An embarrassment really, compared to its resplendent neighbour.

A spindly hand-painted sign above the shack said Caveman Windsurf, which seemed quite apt really. Home to a crusty old sea-dog, a scrawny weather-beaten specimen known unaffectionately as Popeye Hitler.

With a fondness for rum and inhaling herbal remedies, mid-life hadn't been kind to poor old Popeye.

First, his driving license had somehow gotten lost.

He'd heard it would be a full year before it would be found.

Which presented a problem. How to get to work.

A heroine came to his rescue. She got Popeye's pickup, he got a lift. Perfect.

It worked for a while.

But then came the call. The truck had been totalled.

Now lying flat as a pancake, having cartwheeled off the road into mangroves.

It turned out the heroine was rather fond of rum too.

Fortunately, she was fine.

Miraculously.

Poor old Popeye, what was he to do?

An outsider might think he had an idyllic lifestyle, with a leisure business on the beach. No truck now, but still living the dream, how could he possibly be so grouchy?

Allegedly Popeye was a windsurfer, but instead, he

preferred to conduct dawn raids into work on his days off. Then spending his time quaffing Coronas, barking orders and bollocking tourists!

Perhaps it was a chronic case of island fever, a common condition in the Caymans. Generally treated with copious quantities of rum… Or cured for a while with a hop over Hanoi Hannah, who now lived in Havana.

HOWEVER, NOW AND again the island could be a mysteriously treacherous place, perhaps due to its proximity to Hell, which is in fact located not far northwest of Georgetown.

An example was the unfortunate case of a chap called Lucas. A fine fellow old Lucas Clooney. Tash, tan, Ray-Bans, and a real gent.

Would do anything for anyone. But he was somewhat clumsy.

A strange accident occurred and the poor bugger broke his foot. Whilst practising tennis! Luckily being a paramedic he responded quite quickly.

THEN CAME THE Jamaican canoe incident.

Walking the tideline first thing, readying our water-toys for the day, I spotted a five-gallon drum washed up on the sand.

It was sealed. And heavy.

Drugs, I joked back in the shack. Timmy thought a severed head. Obviously.

Prising the top off, a taped-up black bin liner was revealed. Definitely a head, Timmy said.

I cut it open. And found another taped up bag. Drugs. Nah it's a head.

Timmy was wrong.

Shit! get that outta here, screamed Popeye. Hide it behind the sails, don't say a word. I will deal it later. Sorry, I meant to say deal with it later.

After a while, a man wearing dark glasses approached the counter. A very serious looking man, with very dark glasses. Not a tourist, I thought.

Are you the boss? No, but he should be here soon. Can I help?

I'll be back. Said Arnold.

And he was. Quite soon in fact. Still looking very serious, same dark glasses still on.

Sorry, he's still not back. Can I help you?

He showed me a badge. It turned out he wasn't called Arnold.

But he was with the D.E.A, as they say Stateside.

A Jamaican canoe has just been intercepted, but they ejected their cargo, eight bales of ganga, over the side. Have you seen anything?

Oh Fuck.

Errrr no. Do you want to borrow a wave runner to go and look?

Sure, thanks.

No problem, you're welcome.

…Always pleased to help!

SO POPEYE SCORED the lot, and it was a lot.

Apparently, a little was wet, but the rest went in his loft.

There was a problem though. Grand Cayman gets hot, very hot sometimes, and marijuana smells. Strongly, especially when stored in a loft, a rather hot loft.

Smoking it can sometimes also make you paranoid. Allegedly.

Storing twenty pounds of the stuff in a loft above your apartment apparently leads to more paranoia. Popeye got really paranoid.

The weed went back from whence it came. Into the sea. At around 3 a.m!

A CHUBBY FRIENDLY chap named Matt owned the dive shop, helped by an often merry international band of instructors.

A fast-talking Irishman, a well 'ard London Lad, a quiet moonlighting gardener, a tall, skinny, pale, red-faced comic, Swanvesta, and a shapely, tanned Swiss mountain goat called Blacky. A top team. The dream team. Well almost.

Poor Popeye seemed quite jealous of Matt. His team. His expensive dive boats. His sunset cruises.

Popeye only had a paltry collection of ageing, grubby windsurf boards. He only had two cheeky pomms working for him.

Matt had a catamaran as well, crewed by the nimble Swiss mountain goat. They ran snorkel trips, and all smiled a lot too.

What to do? What to do?

Popeye bought a boat. It would be war, he declared. We will copy him, we will beat him. But greed clouded poor Popeye's judgement. Possibly rum too, one suspects.

Back at the counter, a couple approached. Expensive clothes. Jewellery. Makeup. Tourists. I thought. Wealthy too.

Sunset tour? they said.

Absolutely. Over there. Pointing.

Disappointment. Not hidden. At all.

The boat, if you could call it that, lay ploughed bow first onto the beach. Well, I think it was the bow. Difficult to tell really. The boat was ugly. And small.

But it did have a fancy name. Hand-painted of course.

THE MAIDEN VOYAGE was a disaster. First they got lost, and then a reef jumped out in front of them. The steering was at fault, apparently. And then the engine wouldn't start. Foul play was suspected by a fuming Popeye.

Captain Morgan seemed a likely suspect.

I tried to tow the boat back to base, but it was no use, she was taking on water fast. As I got the last passenger safely ashore I looked back, but the boat was in sight no more.

Sunk without a trace.

Of Popeye, there was no sign. A sea-dog to the last,

the skipper had gone down with his ship.

Poor Popeye.

ANY RESEMBLANCE TO real people and actual events is possibly purely coincidental!

But sad to say rumour has it that Popeye still stalks the shores of Cayman, Corona in hand, ranting and bollocking tourists...

Central America
2001

God and Jesus Alive in Guatemala

DAWN AND HEADED for the border. Wedged standing amongst pungent locals, only a thin steel bar prevented passengers from toppling off as we bumped along in the back of an overloaded pickup truck. Lit gold by rising sun, the craggy peaks of a mountain range running parallel helped distract us from the chilly morning air and many discomforts of our cramped journey.

Fortunately, it didn't take too long to reach our destination, but exiting from Honduras took an eternity. When we finally passed through control, we walked a few paces, got stamped into Guatemala and within no time boarded a bus for Chiquimula. Ninety minutes later we stepped off that packed bus, then straight onto another going to Guatemala City. Three and a half wearisome hours later we pulled into the capital, but still had one more ride to endure. Luckily it wasn't a long wait for our final bus of the day, and an hour later we, at last, arrived in Antigua. Eager to ditch backpacks, we started the hunt for somewhere to stay, ending up in a tiny room off a courtyard with a rather incongruous white Cadillac parked in its centre.

Next morning we awoke to find lavish preparations for Semana Santa in full swing. All around the cobbled streets of the old city, long, intricate alfombras were being carefully laid. Made from leaves, petals, seeds and dyed sawdust, these colourful carpets require patience, skill and dedication to create. Artisans lay on planks spanning the road, hand placing materials to make vibrant masterpieces of design and detail. But within hours their painstaking efforts are destroyed by Easter week processions walking over the carpets which stretch around the city.

Eighty men carry a massive platform, or anda, bearing a statue of Christ on the cross, on shoulders around a nine-hour circumnavigation of the city. The combined weight of the ornate platform and statue is a staggering 8500 pounds. Working in shifts, four thousand men bear the statue, systematically replacing each other under the anda as it moves through the narrow streets without stopping.

Dressed in hooded purple robes and veiled by thick clouds of burning incense, with drummers, pipers and tuba players bringing up the rear, the sombre procession sways down alfombra lined streets.

Sometimes the huge cross gets snagged on power lines when helpers wielding poles are too slow in shoving the overhead cables aside. The strain on faces of devotees supporting the colossal weight is evident, yet they pay for the honour of taking part.

Antigua's holy week celebrations are an impressive

spectacle and draw in huge crowds from all over Central America. Each night the alfombras are recreated in preparation for the following day's processions. Dating back almost 500 years to when Spanish conquistadors arrived, the tradition represents the crucifixion. The large sculpture of Christ is itself 350 years old.

SURROUNDED BY THREE imposing volcanoes the beautiful city is in a dramatic setting. Fine colonial architecture lines its cobblestone streets, mixed with crumbling ruins or pastel facades below terracotta roofs. In its markets and main plaza, colourful street traders tempt tourists with trinkets, handicrafts and woven textiles.

Nearby Volcan Pacaya was active, so I made the slow ascent to its summit in pre-dawn darkness and squinted down through eye-burning sulphur clouds to a fiery molten lava lake glowing 200 feet below. It should have been an easy climb but my boots were back in Belize, so I hiked in open-toed Teva sandals. Tiny granules of lava tortured me as they grated and shredded my feet, especially when we scree skied down the cinder cone. As we descended plumes of smoky gases spewed from the volcano and were lit orange by low early morning sun.

FIVE HUNDRED YEARS ago Antigua was Guatemala's capital until the city was flattened by two earthquakes in the late 1700s, leaving behind little but ruins. We explored the devastated remains of a once magnificent church and convent torn apart by the quakes. Massive collapsed sections of stonework gave glimpses of its former glory and stature, just as the jumbled collection of pieces demonstrated the colossal power of the earthquakes. It's a wonder that city dwellers kept their faith after their church was destroyed twice during the same century.

AFTER WATCHING JESUS parade around the streets we decided to go to visit God next, who allegedly lived in a small village near Lago de Atitlan up in the highlands. So we headed for Panajachel, about 150 km from Antigua, aboard yet another bus. The town, also known as Gringo-tenango, has been a favourite hangout for travellers since the hippie days of the 60s and 70s and gained its nickname from locals, which means place of foreigners.

Panajachel is in a sublime setting, nestled on the shores of scenic Lago de Atitlan. Created inside a collapsed volcano, the expansive lake is set amongst verdant rolling hills and overlooked by three large volcanoes. Simple wooden boats ply its waters, ferrying tourists and locals alike between villages sprinkled around the shoreline.

God apparently lived across the lake in a small hut in the Mayan village of Santiago Atitlan. Well, we'd heard he did, but others said it was the Devil who lived there. The Devil God is known as Maximon, or San Simon, a deity revered through the Guatemalan highlands, and is believed to be a combination of Mayan gods and the biblical Judas, representing both light and dark.

AFTER WE TIED up alongside a primitive wooden jetty and walked its wobbling planks ashore, a gang of urchins approached holding out grubby palms for a few quetzales to take us to Maximon. Passing groups of villagers in colourful traditional Mayan clothing, our scuffy ten-year-old guides led us through dirty backstreets until we came to a small dwelling.

Inside, we found three men enshrouded by thick cigarette smoke. One, bent over on his knees, chanted fervently in front of a wooden, scarf-adorned, humanlike effigy wearing a wide-brimmed western hat!

Maximon wore a coat of money, with dollar bills and quetzales stuck all over his dark robe. A long cigarette dangled from his lips. At his feet lay burning candles, bottles of rum and cigarette cartons by the dozen.

Pilgrims and shaman who travel to worship and pray in front of this pagan effigy leave these offerings in hope of improved lives and more worldly goods. Yet it seems the person who gains most from their prayers is Maximons caretaker.

Although with an unlimited supply of free alcohol and nicotine, his prosperous life is perhaps unlikely to be a long one!

Chichicastenango chicken bus

NATURES REPETITIVE, INFURIATING alarm clock roused me reluctantly from a restless slumber. It was four a.m. Far too early to be awake unless you are a cockerel, but it didn't take long before some dogs joined in too. They were probably sick of the damn birds too and, like me, longed to seal their beaks for good.

My mattress wasn't helping either as it was too small and lumpy to lull me back to some much-needed sleep. Soon the relentless roosters had set off every dog in town, and when one stopped barking another would start. I endured predawn dozing in discomfort, dreaming of decapitating chooks and dogs. It wasn't the best start to the day, but annoyingly in this part of the world was fairly normal. Next time I would bring earplugs… Or perhaps a gun!

WITH A LONG, loud blast of its air-horn, the old school bus roared from around the bend amidst a swirling dust storm thrown up from the loose surface. It skidded to a stop, and the fight for seats was on as people tried to shove past a stream of snack vendors and disembarking passengers. Alas, we hadn't been fast or forceful enough. No seats remained.

The driver pulled away, but minutes passed before bodies and luggage were crammed or forced into available spaces. Our bus was stuffed to the seams. Four people stood wedged in its footwell. Two more hung from the open door with toes barely on board, clinging on with death grips. Two and a half hours later we pulled into Uspantan, sweaty, cramped and plastered with road dust. We had covered forty kilometres!

Claire's excellent command of Spanish soon uncovered the depressing fact there would be no further buses until three the next morning. Too early even for cockerels! The prospect was not appealing, and we didn't want to spend an hour, let alone half the night, in the isolated dusty village, so chanced our luck and stayed put on the roadside.

Fortune favoured us as, after a spell, a Toyota pickup showed up, taking us on to Chicaman, where we'd been told we could catch a bus. On arrival, we discovered there was a bus, but it wasn't leaving until four the following morning. It was the same bus! We'd gained nothing but an extra hour in bed.

Faced with little chance of onward travel, we found a rough-looking place serving food and sampled the local speciality: burger and chips! A rare treat amongst the usual endless plates of pollo, arroz y frijoles!

After lunch, with nothing to lose, we stood again by the road, having heard something may be along later. Happily, the vague info turned out to be correct and a cattle truck pulled up early afternoon, headed for San

Cristobal Verapaz, well on the way to Coban.

With vehicles being scarce around these parts, locals and travellers alike use whatever transport is available, and the truck driver was pleased to take fares. There was standing room for plenty, but the spare tyre, fuel barrel and a filthy tarpaulin were the only concessions to passenger comfort in the back of the open truck. With no other takers, I clambered on top of the huge fuel drum. The stench of diesel was strong, but I had an elevated view and somewhere to sit.

Until just a few years ago the route would have been impossible to safely travel as the area had been a guerrilla stronghold during the civil war that ravaged the country for thirty-six years. During that time 200,000 Guatemalans were killed, millions made homeless and untold thousands disappeared. In the eighties, the government implemented a scorched earth policy, and razed over 400 villages, exterminating the population in areas where rebels were thought to be. Anyone who survived the slaughter and torture got rounded up and put into special camps surrounded by army forces. In December 1996 a peace accord was signed ending hostilities and bringing hope for a brighter future to the people.

THE TORTUOUS UNMADE track was in an appalling state with deep holes, ruts, rocks and huge boulders. Often our truck was reduced to walking pace as it wound its way up a perilous mountain slope. With precipitous drops only a foot from his wheels, our driver could take no chances. Twice we passed broken down trucks with wrecked tyres and later picked up some very lucky people, whose pickup veered over the edge when its steering broke.

Conversation in the back was impossible over the deafening laboured roar of an overworked diesel engine and our senses were soon numbed by a constant metallic rattle from broken bars on the trucks steel-caged sides.

The day dragged on with little relief from the racket and discomfort, other than spectacular views enjoyed from the elevation of my stinky steel seat. Now and again, in the middle of nowhere, with not a dwelling in sight, the truck would pull up and a person would alight, before quickly disappearing off the side of the track. Several times we forded fast flowing rock-strewn rivers, praying the engine didn't conk out midstream.

By the time we reached San Cristobal it was almost six, but there was no chance of a break as we jumped straight aboard another old American school bus. Within half an hour the bus had whisked us over smooth paved roads into the small town of Coban.

With its sealed roads, modern shops and locals dressed in western clothes, it felt like we'd arrived in a different world after our past few days of travel. Even with the final fast leg included, today's journeys had taken eight hours to cover less than a hundred miles!

Coban had few attractions, but to break up the tough travelling we explored a nearby forest reserve and bolstered stomach reserves in readiness for our next bus ordeals.

Next morning a public holiday made it a bad day to travel as everyone seemed to be going somewhere. Our bus should have seated 48 and the four bench seats in front of us were each built for three, but I counted 32 people crushed there. Behind, the heads were impossible to count but there looked close to 140 passengers on board! It was yet another long, unpleasant and uncomfortable journey.

Known as chicken buses, for the live cargo that frequently accompanies locals, it's best not to look too closely before you board. These battle-scarred vehicles have endured hard lives, with huge dents, missing lights and smashed off mirrors. Bumpers and body panels are often held on with the help of wire or string. In windscreens dangling crucifixes, Jesus Saviour placards and crazed glass conspire to dangerously obscure the driver's view. And it's never a good idea to even glance at the state of its tyres!

DAYS EARLIER IN the Mayan town of Chichicastenango, its narrow cobbled streets had been almost impassable during the Sunday market that engulfs its plaza and sprawls into surrounding streets. Traders clad in vibrant traditional reds, blues, and yellows contrasted with their ochre ceramics and earthy stoneware stacked neatly at the roadside. Draped tarpaulins shaded colourful displays of carved masks, intended to tempt passing tourists to part with dinero. Young mothers meandered amongst the crowd, arms and shoulders piled with woven textiles for sale and swaddled toddlers bundled on their backs.

The indoor fruit market was another riot of aroma and colour and a scene of much activity. Sacks of fruit and veg by the hundred stood in lines filling floor space, leaving little room for buyers to haggle with traders squatting beside their produce. I climbed stairs above the large hall to shoot photos, but within minutes was forced to leave by a barrage of fruit launched from below! The whole town was stuffed to its seams with shoppers and traders, along with more than a few camera-toting gringo tourists.

AFTER THE BUSTLING chaos of Chichicastenango we hoped for a quieter stay in El Estor, but it wasn't to be. Nestled on the shoreline of Lago de Izabal, Guatemala's largest lake, the setting was serene, even if the streets weren't. The place was packed with tourists, but we seemed to be the only gringos in town. A public holiday had drawn in the crowds, making it tough to find accommodation, but the lengthy search helped stretch our cramped limbs after enduring yet another long bus ride.

Dawn found us puttering across the broad, peaceful lake to explore its pristine Bocas del Polochic reserve. This important wetland covers an area of over 50.000 acres, provides a home to 300 species of birds and is one of the most bio-diverse regions in Guatemala. Sharing our slim wooden boat with only a guide, we'd finally escaped the crowds and could breathe fresh clean air again.

Howler monkeys barked out raucous calls as we cruised along dense tree-lined banks. Hefty silver tarpon swirled by lily-choked margins, as diving manatee left broad tail-prints behind on the calm surface. Blue herons and egrets stalked the shallows, kingfishers flashed by and an array of exotic species swooped overhead. The trip provided a perfect antidote to the previous days of gruelling travelling.

Back on dry land, we discovered that due to the holiday no more buses were running, which meant spending a second night in our hot, noisy hospedaje. On yet another lumpy undersized bed.

"VAMANOS. VAMANOS. RAPIDOS!" Yelled our animated driver, as the last few stragglers scrambled on board. Departure! At last. We'd boarded over half an hour ago and now it seemed we may, at last, start our journey as the overloaded bus pulled away from the plaza. But it wasn't to be. Instead, we drove to a gas station.

Earlier, a near frantic busboy had hustled us aboard in such haste that we had thrown away food we'd been eating. With only one bus leaving today we couldn't risk missing it, so scrabbling to scoop up backpacks we'd run and hurled our luggage inside. A handful of seats remained, so we plonked on the nearest, relieved to have caught the bus. But then we sat there. And sat there. And waited.

Eventually, our driver pulled away, only to take a slow loop around town before coming back to the square where we'd started! His dawdling circuit had been accompanied by much hooting and hollering, hoping to cram even more people aboard. Then we waited. Again.

The bus was now overloaded to bursting point, so was becoming unbearably hot inside, and I was becoming increasingly pissed off by the thought of my wasted breakfast, which was in a nearby bin! Then the busboy decided to collect fares, clasping his bundle of cash as he forced his way through the crush of sweating bodies.

Finally, we pulled away… and went to the gas station.

As our fuel tanks slowly filled, so the passengers continued to slowly cook. Even when they were full, we still didn't get on our way. Instead, we drove to a bus office, where our driver disappeared inside.

By the time we departed I'd already had more than enough, even though these antics were quite normal here. Fortunately a mere ninety minutes later we extracted ourselves from the mobile microwave and escaped into fresh air. We hadn't been confident of an onward link from Rio Dulce, but surprisingly stepped straight onto a luxury coach, and for the first time in the country, I had a single seat all to myself!

By midday, we were climbing steps to a primitive treehouse at Finca Ixobel, a few kilometres from the small town of Poptun. Set amongst pine trees and jungle, this friendly eco-farmstead felt an oasis of calm. It also had a superb buffet which came as a welcome relief from the standard Guatemalan fare of chicken, beans and rice, or chicken, beans, and tortilla for every single meal!

JOINING A SMALL group of travellers we hiked for two hours through thick rainforest to explore an isolated river cave. Near its entrance, we suspended food bags out of reach of rats, tucked clothes out of sight and followed a guide into chilly dark waters.

With limited torch power to light our way we spent the next hours slipping, swimming or wading through a series of large caverns. The snaking river led us past strange alien collections of glistening stalagmites and stalactites, beneath colonies of hanging fruit bats. Then the tunnel ended at a large rock. Below was a black void that our feeble lamps couldn't penetrate, but that didn't prevent the guide from launching himself off! A moment later came the sound of a loud splash, then his voice encouraging us to follow. It took blind trust to plunge into the unseen pool below.

Outside in daylight our food and clothes were found unmolested, so enjoyed a lazy lunch as the sun re-warmed our bodies, before the slow wander back to base.

Back in our treehouse, we discovered unwelcome squatters in the shape of several huge spiders. Uncertain of their species and wary of their size, they demanded careful eviction, especially at night as our treehouse had no lights. Persistent mosquitoes kept us awake most of the first night, then I spent three days picking a hundred tiny ticks off my body. An unwanted souvenir from the cave hike!

We were heading for Tikal, so after a brief restful stay at the Finca, hit the road again, taking a bus first to Flores, then to El Remate on the shores of Lago Peten Itza.

Gazing from our open-sided roof-terrace room in a hostel, the only activity in this sleepy spot was provided by small processions of chickens, dogs or pigs that paraded past at intervals during the day!

THE BUS FOR Tikal departed at five a.m, but that presented little problem as ever-present cockerels gave us an early alarm call, and soon we were hiking into jungle hearing alarm calls of far more exotic species.

Buried deep in rainforest, Tikal is an imposing complex of temples and monuments once inhabited by the Mayan civilisation. Thought to be the most important city in their empire, the area was first settled in 900 B.C. The city grew through the centuries to a peak in 8 A.D. when its population reached 100,000. For unknown reasons the Mayan empire collapsed the following century, leaving Tikal abandoned, allowing jungle to reclaim the site.

For a thousand years, the ancient city was lost to the world until an expedition discovered ruins in 1848, starting the battle of reclaiming its stonework back from the jungle.

OVERHEAD, A THICK canopy sounded alive with roaring

howler monkeys and screeching parrots as we took a meandering path through trees. On the ground, coatimundis scurried across the track before disappearing into dense undergrowth.

Climbing the great pyramid of El Mundo Perdido, we emerged on its summit and shared the magical moment with a handful of people. Gazing out over lush canopy as early mists dissipated, only jutting peaks of temples interrupted the endless green panorama spread beneath us. Intoxicating sounds wafted up and enveloped us as we watched macaws and toucans work treetops below. Towering dead trees, with heavy boughs bearing swathes of spiky primitive air plants further enhanced the sensation of being in The Lost World.

Tikal covers a huge area and contains 3000 structures, the tallest of which is Temple Four at over 60 metres. To preserve its stonework, a wooden tower with countless zigzagging steps had been constructed, presenting quite a climb in the heat. But our reward for the relentless slog was worth it as we sat like Mayan rulers, bathed in sunlight, surveying the sprawling scene beneath our feet.

Facing each other like towering bookends are the majestic temples of the Grand Plaza. We climbed massive stone steps up Temple Two and sat looking back towards Temple One, built to bury and honour King Moon Double Comb. When excavated, his tomb was found to contain hundreds of intricately carved objects of bone and jade jewellery. King Moon had been a powerful leader and is thought to have built many of the surviving temples during his fifty-year rule.

As the day grew older a few arriving tour groups disturbed the tranquillity, but even they could do little to detract from our visit due to the sheer scale of the site.

Tikal's imposing temples are enhanced by flat, parched plazas at their feet, and the blackened limestone structures stand out against lush rainforest encircling the remote site. With little human disturbance, an exotic jungle soundtrack and a spectacular natural setting, visiting the ancient ruins was an enchanting experience.

TIKAL IS CLOSE to Belize and the last stop on our circuitous tour of Guatemala, so later that day we climbed into yet another bus and crossed over the border. Two further buses took us back to Belize City. I collected the kit I'd left in a guesthouse, then climbed aboard a jet bound for L.A.

Central America had certainly been an adventure, but I was glad to be leaving its beds, cockerels and, especially, buses behind. And I couldn't wait to eat something other than pollo, arroz y frijoles!

Vietnam and Cambodia 2016

A day in Danang

SIX A.M. AND I'm strolling white sand along China beach which stretches south towards Hoi An. Already it's busy with bathers splashing in surf and barefooted joggers by the shoreline.

A cluster of hopeful fishermen work from simple coracles, whilst more wade the shallows hauling nylon nets ashore. A small crowd gathers, curious to see their catch of glistening silver fish. Higher up the beach, others practice Tai chi. Some lying stretched face down in soft sand, others balanced, bizarrely, on their heads! Then there are the comical rotisserie tanners, arms outstretched calmly pirouetting under the early sun!

I HIRE A bike and head west towards the Han River but soon discover my brakes barely work and the handlebars are loose. Neither would be a worry if the traffic wasn't so crazy. But here, four lanes multiply into ten, teeming with thousands of overloaded scooters.

I spot a family of five squeezed onto one. A huge sack of rice balanced on the rear of another, and a metal table held one-handed by the rider on yet another. An eight-foot-tall orange tree glides sedately past! Then a long ladder, followed by a dozen water barrels fixed somehow to a different scooter. A big sheet of glass passes by, propped, insanely, between rider and his glove-less pillion.

Later, I'm slowly overtaken by several metres of scaffold pole, before the scooter, rider and last few metres of pole go past! Despite the ridiculous, precariously balanced loads and relentless volume of traffic, some riders are busy texting.

Reaching a roundabout with a crossing I stop, but no one else does. The traffic is truly chaotic with scooters coming from every direction and dozens of riders going against the flow. Nobody stops, yet somehow everyone squeezes or weaves a way through. It's amazing, alarming, funny and frustrating all at the same time!

Arriving at the immense Dragon bridge spanning Han River I cycle under its huge golden head which breathes fire and water, but only on weekends! Following the river, I pedal towards a fleet of primitive wooden fishing boats lying at anchor and spot a bloated pig washed up on the bank. Perhaps it was preferable to take a short swim rather than be chopped up and put in a pot!

BACK IN MY fourth-floor room in the Moonshine Hotel, I peer through concrete spattered glass and notice a new pile of bricks on the tower block being built a foot away and realise tomorrow my sea view will be no more!

Danang is a city under construction and its daily soundtrack is now in full swing. A relentless racket of hammer blows and clattering scaffold poles compete with a constant background chorus of car and scooter horns. Sometimes the cacophony is briefly interrupted by metallic calls of buhp dai, buhp dai, bursting from a nearby bike mounted corn sellers megaphone.

Despite my jet-lag, the discordant, clamorous din allows me little chance to doze… maybe it's time to hit that beach once more!

Hiding near Hue
(pronounced Haway)

HUE. HOME TO roaming hordes of hawkers and tourist touts.

Ever present, ever hopeful, ever vocal.

Calling: Hello taxi. Hello?

Hello, cyclo. Hello?

Hustling: Very cheap. Hello? Hello!

At night. Whispering from the shadows: Lady? Lady? Very cheap. Very beautiful!

Walking away. Mañana amigo. Mañana.

Sometimes that works. Sometimes they follow.

I take you there. For one dollar. Only one dollar. Very beautiful…

LEAVING HOTEL HUE Nino behind I tire of the noise, and the street slalom around the people, the potholes, the stalls and the endless scooters.

Seeking the serenity of water, I head for the Perfume River which bisects the city.

Hello riverboat. Hello!

Very cheap. Only fifty thousand. One hour. Hello?

Thank you, no. Thank you. No!

I keep walking, but don't get far.

Hello riverboat. Hello. Very cheap…

I run the gauntlet and make it as far as the bridge.

Hello motorbike! Hello. Where you go?

Pointing. That way. Over the bridge.

I walk on and escape across the river.

Ducking into a street market I'm met with a chaotic bustle of people, produce and yet more scooters.

Stallholders squatting on the street, produce spread enticingly around them, locals shopping fresh, laden scooters attempting to squeeze through.

Hello. Hello! Looking? Very cheap…

I EXIT THE market and retreat to the main road, risking a crossing in the relentless flow. Walking at a slow but steady pace I step into the road and let the traffic part around me, scooters and cars weaving past on both sides, hoping and praying that everyone else is paying attention.

Unquestionably unnerving, but utterly necessary as nobody stops for pedestrians, who rank little higher than dogs in the highway pecking order here.

HUGGING THE STREET edge I hike to the Citadel, a vast historic Imperial Enclosure sprinkled with imposing palaces and pagodas.

Built around 200 years ago to house the Emperor and his ruling dynasty, it now seems to act mainly as a tranquil haven for tourists hiding from the cities tireless touts!

Peace at last.

Dong Ha and the DMZ

THE GUIDEBOOK SAID excellent, but it certainly wasn't.

New backpackers HQ the page had read, but the place was old.

And it was empty.

There were plenty of the hotels business cards though.

Showing a brand new building with a Porsche parked outside!

The stair layout was lethal, I tripped and grabbed for the rail.

But it came off the wall in my hands!

Upstairs in my room, was a single curtain.

I drew it back carefully but the pole fell and clouted me on the head!

It hurt. But only a little.

The bed frame was made from wood. And so it seemed was my mattress.

But it did have a small human shaped dent in the middle.

Laying atop the wooden bed was a garish thin blanket.

Which must have been woven by a blind person.

But it looked fine with the light switched off.

This excellent new hotel was built right beside a busy main road.

Great for scooter watching. But not so great for sleep.

Four hours is fine I thought, as I stumbled down the stairs around dawn.

In search of caffeine to help sustain the lie.

It worked for a while…

THE GUIDE WAS called Hwa and he claimed to have borrowed the car.

But it seemed somewhat unlikely unless the owner had never seen him drive.

Perhaps he had simply stolen it.

Being a guide though, he did seem to know the way.

But he didn't know how to drive.

Well, perhaps in theory he did, he just had no concept of safety.

Being a passenger was really quite scary.

Hwa said he was a veteran of the American war in Vietnam.

But I wasn't sure any of us would actually survive the day.

It would have been the ultimate irony; a Viet. vet. showing tourists around a battle zone that he had survived, only to be taken out by a truck…

Hwa seemed unsure if his glasses helped.

So he tried them on for a spell, then took them off again.

Then back on again they went. And off again.

Whilst erratically weaving along the road.

And having the cheek to complain about scooter rider's behaviour.

He truly was dangerous.

Worryingly so on these roads where nine thousand die each year.

Which equates to twenty-five people every single day.

Leaving the car running on a blind crest we went to look for a tank and found the fifty-year-old relic half buried in bushes.

I was hoping we would also find the car still in its spot.

Which contained my backpack…

HAMBURGER HILL TURNED out a little disappointing, we couldn't even get lunch, and Camp Carroll was apparently away at a drag show.

The bridge over Ben Hai River dividing North and South got destroyed by B52's but was rebuilt for tourists, so we walked across.

Very convenient!

AND THEN THERE was the graveyard.

One of seventy-two in the province.

Containing eleven thousand dead Vietnamese in this one alone.

Lines of white headstones, stretching over the hillside. Everywhere.

Hundreds simply marked martyr. Unidentified remains.

Multiple mass graves. Bones recovered from jungle.

Unknown soldiers. Unknown people. Bones mixed with bones.

Seventy two graveyards just in this province alone.

Three hundred thousand bodies still missing.

Unrecovered.

AND THEN THERE is the unexploded ordnance.

A daily danger and reality for those living and working here.

Fifty years on after the American war, and still people are losing their lives every day. Or being hideously maimed.

Fifty years on.

The DMZ had an unimaginable fourteen million tonnes of ordnance dropped on it.

A third of that is thought to be still lying around unexploded.

One hundred thousand innocent civilian lives have been lost since the conflict ended.

Every year that count rises.

CREATED IN 1954 as a buffer zone between North and South Vietnam the area saw some of the bloodiest battles and heaviest fighting and got bombed relentlessly.

The DMZ is located in the narrowest part of the country, and the heavy bombing massively disrupted supplies from the north through the bottleneck. In response the NVA sent ten times the quantity that was needed, knowing that only ten percent would arrive safely.

In Phong Nha to the north big rafts were built to create floating bridges. Stored in river caves by day they came out under cover of darkness to move vehicles and supplies.

LATER, HWA TOOK us to visit the Vinh Moc tunnels, a vast underground network of narrow passages on three levels down to depths of twenty-three metres. Housing up to ninety families in two kilometres of hand-dug tunnels, with living spaces, cooking chambers, latrines, a well, even a hospital. An absolute labyrinth.

Fortunately, it was impossible to imagine the terror of being inside the tunnels during a bombing raid, and I couldn't decide which would have been worse, being bombed above ground, or cowering deep underground and hearing a drilling bomb coming closer.

The maze of passages had multiple entrances, air shafts, vents and openings on the coast for bringing in supplies. Above ground, waist deep trenches linked entrances, and I was glad to see those again after spending a claustrophobic hour exploring underground.

BACK ON THE road, the sobering experience hadn't improved Hwa's driving skills.

At one point I shouted NO! to stop him attempting a suicidal overtake.

Luckily he listened and swerved back in as the on-coming truck blazed by.

How he made it through the conflict I do not know…

Driving on the right... but usually being in the wrong!

EXTRACTS FROM THE Vietnamese Driving Test:

On a fast straight road you catch up with a slow-moving truck just before the brow of a blind crest. Would you:
a.   Slow down?
b.   Maintain your speed, beep constantly and overtake it regardless?

Approaching a blind bend with three slower scooters riding abreast in front of you. Do you:
a.   Slow down behind the scooters?
b.   Beep constantly, stay at the same speed and swerve around them on the bend?

Coming to a T junction where you want to turn left, the driver in front surprisingly uses his indicators and signals left. Do you:
a.   Maintain road position, slow down and follow?
b.   Beep aggressively, then overtake him on the inside, cutting off the whole corner and forcing your way across oncoming traffic with frantic use

the car horn?

Driving an ambulance, but not during an emergency, you catch up with a slower scooter but there is an oncoming tourist on a bicycle. Would you:

a. Slow down until the cyclist passed?
b. Beep loudly and overtake the scooter, forcing the tourist off the road into a ditch?

Whilst riding home by scooter with three young children on the back, you spot a friend on the opposite side of the road. Do you:

a. Pull off the main road to safely park your scooter?
b. Stop right in the centre for a good old chat?

It's the wet season and is pouring down again but you have to ride to work. Would you:

a. Put on your waterproofs?
b. Ride along holding out an umbrella to shield your face, looking sideways with just an occasional peek over the top to see where you are going?

Aboard your scooter, you are coming towards a busy five-way junction. Do you:

a. Slow, and approach with caution?
b. Continue to look down at your phone, meander into the junction and just hope that everyone misses you?

You and some friends have been logging trees in the forest. Would you:

a. Leave the thick trunks to be collected later by truck?

b. Balance three-metre long sections across the seats of your scooters and ride home?

Finally, when navigating the hectic, chaotic streets of the capital what protective equipment would be appropriate wear aboard your scooter:

a. Helmet and gloves. And hopefully boots, jeans and a jacket?

b. Flip-flops, a dust mask, football shorts and earplugs!

THIS IS FICTIONAL, of course, as it seems unlikely there is any sort of driving test in Vietnam. However, if you answered b to all the above, you will fit in just fine!

Having witnessed all these instances, and countless others every day, it's little wonder that Vietnam has such an appalling road death record.

ON MY SECOND day in the country, a fast-moving scooter missed me by a millisecond going flat out in the wrong direction down a split dual carriageway. For ten minutes I'd been walking along a pavement with two busy lanes coming towards me, waiting for a gap in the flow. I saw my chance to cross and stepped off the curb. The moped flashed past from behind, missing me by inches. The rider was travelling so fast and was so close he didn't even have time to swerve.

One more step and I wouldn't be writing this story. But it taught me an essential early survival lesson for Vietnam!

Caving in Phong Nha

IN THE SULTRY afternoon heat, a small wooden sign which said Pub with Cold Beer came as a welcoming sight. I'd left the village behind hours ago and at first, cycled the tranquil banks of Son River. Midstream, fisherman harvested weed from its shallow waters standing in long, low-slung boats with lengths of bamboo.

A group of backpackers had left their bikes by the roadside and a Vietnamese lad was helping himself to one. I shouted and gesticulated, but he just grinned and cycled past. I found the riders and together we ran to the road, by which time the still grinning lad was coming back on the bike. It seemed he'd only borrowed it to fetch a machete, and with a cheeky smile handed the bike back over!

Freewheeling further, I passed lush rice paddies worked by mud-baked water buffalo and crouched farmers beneath simple conical hats. Orange-tinged dirt tracks led through a serene rural landscape that looked untouched by time. The handful of faces I saw were friendly, waving, smiling or calling "Xin Chao!".

Arriving at Phong Nha Farmstay I sampled their Huda beer and met the owner who told me I'd just missed some Hollywood stars, who'd been filming scenes for Kong Skull Island only the week before.

Backtracking through the peaceful paddies I pushed on for the main road. The sun was high and the heat getting oppressive, so I felt pleased to see the pub sign promising more cold beer.

A rough dirt track led off into fields and would have been fun on a mountain bike, but mine was equipped with a low seat, no suspension, and a large basket up front! The prospect of icy beer motivated me to keep pedalling down the lonely potholed track until an isolated building came into view. Large letters above a stone archway announced it actually was called The Pub with Cold Beer!

As I rode into the courtyard a woman rushed towards me and asked if I wanted to share a chicken! Apparently, the near-deserted farmlike pub sold barbequed chicken as well as cold beer, and Lena had been hoping someone would show up to share a freshly cooked one with her. Hot chook with cold beer sounded fine, so our host chased and caught us one. Then he wrung its neck, defeathered the foul and flung it onto his fire!

My chilled beer went down a treat, and the super fresh chicken was fantastic.

THE DAY WAS getting on, so when I got back to the main road, chose a direct route to Son Trach along tarmac. The fast road had little traffic, but halfway back an ambulance came towards me at speed. It was fast catching a slower scooter but not using sirens or flashing lights. As the rider drew closer, I assumed the ambulance driver would slow, but instead, he swerved fast and wide forcing me off the road and straight into a ditch!

NEXT MORNING I stepped aboard the worn wooden planks of a blue and yellow painted Dragon boat and ventured onto Son River's still, jade waters. Motoring downstream, jagged, mist-enshrouded limestone karsts backdropped verdant banks lined with clusters of long slender boats. When we neared a gaping cave mouth at a cliff base, our skipper cut the engine, and we slipped silently inside. From then, only two paddles propelled our small craft, one to the fore and one aft.

As artificial light replaced daylight, I lay on my back in the bow and gazed in wonder as the otherworldly cave roof glided by. Our Dragon boat slid through smooth inky waters until we came to a beach where we stepped off to explore the immense cave by foot. Stretching underground for eight kilometres, in places the river cave reaches 40 metres in height and is home to hundreds of spectacular stalagmites and stalactites.

Stalactites resembling teeth once guarded its mouth giving the name Phong Nha, or cave of teeth, but during the war, the huge cavern acted as an ammunition dump and was bombed so heavily the teeth didn't survive. Black ugly blast marks still scar the rock face around its entrance.

Phong Nha-Ke Bang National Park is also home to

the world's largest cave; Hang Son Doong, or mountain river cave. A cave so colossal that a 747 could fly through it, and which contains stalagmites that tower to 80 metres. Discovered in 2009 the cave has only been commercially accessible for three years and already there's a seven-month waiting list to see it. I had but a few days to spare, plus the six-day expedition came with a price tag of $3000!

Instead, I settled for a two-day adventure to the Tu Lan cave complex with Oxalis. In comparison, the price was a bargain at a mere five and a half million dong! Equating to less than a tenth of the cost.

LEAVING SON TRACH we drove deserted roads winding through untamed, vegetation draped karst landscapes until we reached the tiny village of Tan Hoa. Here we collected hardhats and head-torches, loaded our dry-packs, then set off on the trek.

Walking through green fields surrounded by spectacular karst scenery, the route skirted past wide-horned water buffalo, and crops of peanut and corn, before leading to Rao Nan River.

Removing boots we splashed through warm shallows to the far bank before making a rocky climb to a small opening into the jungle. From there, a narrow trail wound its way down through a densely vegetated valley. Overhead, the thick canopy shielded faces from strong sun as we tried to protect our hands and arms from a plethora of sharp, spiky and poisonous plants.

Wet underfoot conditions made the infrequently used track ever more challenging, as we wove through treacherous tangles of roots, straddled broad fallen trunks, and scrambled up slippery rocky ascents.

At midday, we stopped inside the mouth of a small cave for lunch, before a sweat making climb led us over Mango mountain and down into Tu Lan valley. A few sticky hours later the sight of tents by a river brought smiles as it meant it was time for a rest or a much-needed swim. With our jungle camp ready set up, all we had to do was ditch our packs, change, then jump into cooling waters cascading from a cave.

Swimming upstream to the waterfall's base, a powerful current surged from its pounding foamy water. Above our heads, cliff face rose hundreds of feet, sprouting clumps of foliage clinging tenaciously to the sheer rock. On a sandbank, a cluster of small tents and hammocks strung under lofty trees made up our secluded, spectacular campsite.

Later, we clambered over huge boulders into Ken cave, eased ourselves into its dark waters and swum upstream into a gaping cavern. As we probed deeper, dangling roots and stalactites became silhouetted against the lush outside world. Fat water droplets splashed down from high above, dappling the surface and echoing around the chamber.

Daylight faded behind us and as the cavern drew darker, torches revealed strange but stunning limestone formations created millennia ago. Exploring further we stepped from its cool water and climbed higher into the underground chamber, squeezing past glistening stalagmites and alien-like structures. Slipping later back into the river, we drifted with current to the cave mouth and returned to a different world warmed by the sun.

Darkness fell quickly and after enjoying a feast around a campfire, I retired to my tent. As the last voices faded exotic jungle noises surrounded our remote camp, but the soothing sound of water soon lulled me into a deep sleep.

NEXT MORNING OUR adventure continued as we pushed into the heart of the Tu Lan system, swimming first into the mouth of a three-million-year-old cavern.

Exploring these underground cathedrals was like entering another world. Weird and wonderful calcite formations created massive cascading chandeliers, huge hanging veils and towering masterpieces resembling melted wax. Collapsed roofs allowed in shafts of sunlight and were fringed with damp mosses and fresh leafy ferns. Mounds of algae covered boulders spilled down jumbled slopes and onto the cave floor.

In places, shallow terraced pools trapped collections of white cave pearls. These polished, pearl-like balls are formed in a similar way to stalagmites, except the calcite accumulates around a nucleus, such as a sand grain, and when agitated by water the pearl grows.

Outside in dense humid jungle, we hiked through deep underfoot leaf litter, weaving through overgrown trails in challenging terrain. We swam in secret blue lagoons, floated downriver on fast stretches of shallows, then enjoyed lunch beside a spectacular waterfall.

All too soon time slipped away and after navigating a dry cave, we climbed a long, near-vertical wooden ladder to the surface and started a reluctant trek back to Tan Hoa. Emerging from the steamy jungle into blazing sunlight we soaked muddy boots and sweating bodies in the river before setting out on the final stretch.

I felt sad to be returning so soon to civilisation, but took some consolation from the thought that each step led me closer to a cold Huda beer!

Cat Ba Island

SOARING LAZILY OVERHEAD a solitary sea eagle surveys the bay in search of a sashimi breakfast.

Below, two fishermen work the shoreline, beating the surface as they row trying to drive fish into their waiting net.

A tiny wooden craft carves a line with its wake as the pilot steers a course between the colourful moored fleet. The slow staccato beat of its ancient outboard drifts in over softer sounds of lapping water.

A larger, more powerful tour boat arrives and nudges up to a jetty, the crew hopeful of more tourist dollars today.

Aboard a huddle of red tin roofed floating restaurants little stirs, aside from gold star national flags flicking in the breeze as the structures rise imperceptibly on an incoming tide.

Ashore, the first scooters are on the street, as vendors languidly lay out collections of tiny blue or red stools in readiness for the day's customers.

Slowly, the sleepy harbour of Cat Ba comes to life…

The Fisherman

Oar blades lie dormant in the water.

The hull moves, undulating on the placid morning swell.

The man is seated, a dark silhouette against the grey
water.

Above him, for shade, a slither of orange.

A simple tiller astern. A hint of blue on the bow.

In one hand he holds a line, with his other, he tweaks an
oar.

The man has nothing in the tiny boat.

But he has knowledge in his head.

Knowledge of these waters.

Passed to him by his father.

And from his father's forefathers.

The man has skill, he is focused.

The man is patient, time is his friend.

Alone on the water, a small presence in the expanse.

The fishermen waits…

Tom Tom Corner

IN THE HEART of Hanoi's cramped and congested old quarter, the wrought iron balconies of Cafe Com Ga overlook the chaotic five-way junction of Cau Dong and Hang Ga. Below, lies a microcosm of life on the bustling streets of the capital.

Traffic here is constant and the noise unrelenting. To even attempt to count the number of scooters would be futile, but just sometimes it may be possible to count a few seconds between the sound of horns!

Buses and bicycles compete with carts and cyclos, as taxis, Toyota's and tuk-tuks try to outmanoeuvre thousands of swarming scooters. An underlying sound-track of traffic and two-stroke engines is overlaid with the urgent beeping of hundreds of horns, creating a ceaseless cacophony. Indicators, lights and even helmets may be considered unnecessary, but one hand or a thumb on the hooter is mandatory!

Flanking the constricted junction a jumbled assort-ment of tube houses crowd the street shouldering for space, squeezed together, piled high and topped with painted tin roofs. Encaged by mesh steel security their deep balconies resemble giant bird cages. Neglected jungles of greenery sprout or cascade from some, others containing little more than drying washing and coloured plastic micro stools.

Built originally to avoid taxes, the narrowest of these tube houses are barely three metres wide but home a huge array of businesses, their overflowing stock stretching back behind the narrow facades. Above striped canopies, grime-coated walls are disguised by draping swathes of thick power cables, congregating in crazy tangles at every pylon.

Pavements everywhere in this crowded city are covered with parked scooters, but not on the corners. Each day Tom Tom corner is a timeshare home to Madam Lan. Squatting beside a huge cauldron of bubbling oil and surrounded by tiny plastic stools she deep fries corn fritters on the pavement. Her cheap but tasty snacks always popular with passers-by.

Close to another corner, Quan and comrades have commandeered a quadrant of space. His business scrubbing scooters is in full swing. A steady trickle of trade arrives as the stream of dirty water flows away. Two little old ladies occupy yet another spot, their heads just visible over a neat array of exotic fruit.

THREE HUGE BLASTS of an air horn announce the arrival of a city bus, recklessly using its size to bully everything before it, forcing a way forward regardless.

A scooter weaves by, a family of five somehow squeezed onto its seat, the toddler in front standing, his tiny chin propped on the speedo. A procession of cyclos sedately glides past. Pink parasols and plastic protecting the pasty, overweight camera-toting tourists.

And all the while traffic flows relentlessly from every direction, and yet hardly anyone ever stops. It appears absolutely chaotic.

Many riders barely seem to be paying attention, with hands in pockets or looking down at phones. No part of road or even pavement goes unused. Riders head against the flow on the wrong side of the road. Others not bothering to slow as they shoot across from side streets, instead simply beeping more. Turning taxis push their way through with blaring horns, forcing multiple minor detours. Somehow everyone makes it through. Most of the time.

Amidst the chaos a giggling backpacker lets out a loud squeal as she dashes across, sidestepping a stray cab. Later the junction is gridlocked as a police van pulls an impromptu U-turn right in the middle. Then the sound of a siren rises above the racket, but it makes little difference to the ambulance's progress. Perhaps if the driver had remembered to switch on his lights, it may have helped!

DESPITE THE VOLUME of traffic, local pedestrians cross without a care. A crisp-white-shirted young dude ambles up the middle, head down, too cool to be troubled by traffic.

Just visible between two basket borne stacks of cardboard a Vietnamese girl, bamboo yoke on shoulder, walks out and lets the traffic part around her. Meanwhile, newly arrived nervous tourists take tentative steps onto the tarmac before retreating once more.

A primitive cart piled high with glittering, gaudy trinkets is pushed into view. Scraping a living on the streets the old lady labours by in her thin-soled sandals and conical straw hat.

A modern-day jouster, his steed a scooter, has twenty feet of bamboo balanced on a shoulder. Tonight there are no challengers and he passes without incident. A shiny, shrink-wrapped coffin crosses, bouncing in the back of a tuk-tuk, its driver perhaps hopeful of some trade following the jouster!

The later it gets the larger the loads ferried by delivery lads. Fixed to the rear of the seat by a single rope at best, but more often just balanced or held by a casual hand over the shoulder. A massive speaker fills the seat on one scooter, somehow also carrying three people. The rear pillion perched on the rack appearing to be floating mid-air, his flip-flops dangling.

Midnight is not long away and life around the junction, at last, begins to slow. Across the street, the lights go out and white shutters slide down at Tom Tom. Off to the side Lan Tan, Tu Van and Lucy Tran have closed, and Quan and co. have long since gone. Madame Lan counts her cash for the last time and then also heads for home.

The day may be drawing to a close, but with the ever-present hordes of scooters still on the street, Hanoi's Tom Tom corner never really sleeps...

Temples, Thieves
and Tuk-Tuks

SEATED ENCIRCLED BY shade from the huge tree erupting between roofs spread below, a sharp bang jolted me from my thoughts as a falling avocado thumped onto a corrugated roof, rattled down a channel, then rolled off again. Despite the shade, the temperature was oppressive and the roof-terraces floor tiles were radiating so much heat I felt my toes being toasted through the soles of my Teva sandals. It was time to stay put, sit still and contemplate the past days in Cambodia.

In the capital Phnom Penh, a city dominated by temples and pagodas, I'd explored the opulent Royal Palace; official residence of the King. Its spectacular Throne Hall is a stunning example of Khmer architecture with ostentatious gilded roofs and an elaborate, slender spire rising to 60m. A life-size solid gold Buddha encrusted with 2000 diamonds resides inside the Silver Pagoda where the floor is laid with 500 pure silver tiles each weighing a kilo.

Collections of bejewelled objects, intricate masks and carvings fill the ornate royal buildings showing the extraordinary skill of Khmer artisans of old. Many parts are closed to the public, but it's possible to amble areas of manicured garden past flamboyant fan palms and admire richly painted walls covered with folklore murals.

WHEN I ARRIVED in Siem Reap aboard a Mekong Express bus from Phnom Penh, a tuk-tuk driver wearing a Mekong company shirt approached. Perfect, I thought, he ought to be trustworthy, but no sooner had we agreed on a price, the now obviously fake t-shirt came off and got stuffed out of sight. So much for that then!

Swinging my backpack inside I climbed aboard, the streets were busy, but the driver squeezed and weaved his narrow tuk-tuk through the traffic towards the Ivy Guesthouse.

The Ivy is close to Siem Reap river with its many fine bridges, so after checking in, I followed its sleepy course towards the touristic maze of Old Market, exploring yet more temples along the way. After dinner, another tuk-tuk driver drove me through unlit backstreets to a big top tent where Phare perform.

The young troupe is Cambodia's answer to Cirque du Soleil and mix astounding acrobatics with performing arts. Accompanied by a band of musicians, a handful of hugely talented artists displayed incredible acts of balance, strength and agility as they enacted their stories. The big top was actually quite small, enabling me to sit just metres from the amazing somersaulting stars of the show.

With a promise of an over-inflated tourist fare, my

teenaged tuk-tuk driver was waiting at the end of the performance and soon dropped me back where I'd started from. But now, after only a few hours the place looked unrecognisable from when I saw it last.

Pub Street had become a heaving mass of partying people, hemmed between packed restaurants and bars on either side. Bobbing heads stretched the length of the street, music belted out and water showered from balconies above. Clouds of flour filled the night as handfuls of the fine powder were flung about in traditional Khmer New Year celebration. Revellers were soaked to the skin and plastered white with dripping flour. It was a riotous scene.

Deciding the balcony in a nearby bar would be a good place to watch, I pushed through the crowd trying to duck the worst of the water being launched by the bucket load from above. But by the time I made it inside my t-shirt was soggy and face and shoulders covered with flour, so with an ice-cold Angkor beer in hand, I climbed to the sanctuary of a balcony and watched the frenzied party rage on below.

Despite the strong temptation to stay and drink, I had to be up for a pre-dawn start next day and knew as a westerner I'd be a target for pickpockets, so would need to keep my wits about me when I left.

Back on the street, I eased into the throng but the crush of hundreds of people made it hard to move, so with hands covering my pockets, I bumped along making progress whenever I could. The atmosphere was electric and the music infectious. I threw up my arms to dance, but instantly felt hands at my pockets.

Slamming my hands down I pushed forward and didn't look back. I was a foreigner surrounded by a sea of unknown faces and couldn't risk trouble trapped in a crowd. It felt like my possessions were still there, so once the people thinned I picked up my pace and headed straight to the guest house.

Knowing I would be a target I'd taken the precaution of using safety pins to secure pockets, and this saved my camera, phone and wallet from being stolen. The pickpocket had undone two press studs in an instant before I felt his hands, but four small pins had prevented disaster.

IT WAS AROUND four thirty when I picked my way along a broad stone causeway towards the temple, feeling pleased an early start had paid off as I followed a couple of flickering torches. Descended stone steps I soon came to a large lily pool and sat down on the shoreline to await sunrise. Behind still waters stretched the wide expanse of temple, but darkness made it difficult to make out much.

As I waited, the area filled with increasingly more tourists, few of whom shared my desire to enjoy the early morning serenity in silence at this special site. When sunlight crept over the horizon, the spectacular silhouette of Angkor Wat gradually came into sharper focus revealing more detail of its intricate stonework.

The sun was still hidden as I climbed steps into the

complex, planning to beat crowds all waiting to take the same sunrise shot behind the pond. Others had shared my idea, but it wasn't too busy inside, leaving me to explore the huge temple without the hordes of excitable Asians.

Built almost 900 years ago to honour Hindu god Vishnu, Angkor Wat is one of the world's biggest religious monuments at 800 metres wide. To gain favour with gods, successive Khmer kings created ever more lavish temples, not as places of religious congregation, but as homes for the gods. It's thought the huge stone complex took 30 years to construct and involved a labour force of 300,000 workers.

The massive site is believed to represent the universe in miniature. At its centre, a sculpted, lotus bud tower soars to 200 metres and represents Mt Meru, mythical home to Hindu gods. Four more majestic towers replicate surrounding peaks and the corners of the world.

Between the towers lie courtyards, chambers and covered galleries set on different levels and linked by stairways. These represent continents and are enclosed behind by an intricately carved corridor lined with 1200 metres of bas-reliefs. Well away from the temple a 200-metre wide square moat represents oceans. Beyond that, thousands of acres of sweltering tropical forest surround the Angkor site.

ANGKOR WAT IS only one part of a vast complex of temples spread amongst tranquil tangled forests. The stone ruins are remnants of an ancient city once the centre of the Khmer Empire, which at its zenith was home to a million people. At that time London had a population of fifty thousand at most.

For a few dollars and the price of an entry ticket, it's possible to hire a personal tuk-tuk driver to transport you between temples. So I spent three days exploring the awe-inspiring site following the footsteps of Lara Croft in Tomb Raider, which had several scenes shot here.

In contrast to well preserved Angkor Wat, at Ta Prohm, jungle has partly reclaimed the site and immense trees stand amongst the impressive ruins. Colossal roots engulf and squeeze its carved stonework before erupting skywards into towering giants. High above, shady canopy conceals birds whose exotic calls penetrate the forest enhancing a feeling of being within an ancient lost world.

After exploring temples, I would find my trusty driver parked in shade dozing in the back of his tuk-tuk. In sweltering heat, the primitive open-sided vehicle provided a perfect way to get around the ruins and dodge crowds.

WITH TIME RUNNING short and an absence of available buses, I flew back to Phnom Penh, and from there caught a bus to Vietnam. After spending an eternity in a vague queue at the border, a lethargic official called my name and re-entering the country proved straightforward. Two hours later I got back to Saigon and checked into a guesthouse in Pham Ngu Lao; an area crowded with busy restaurants and bars. The perfect place to fill up with delicious local food and a final few Huda beers before a reluctant return to the UK.

On my last day, I took a taxi to the airport to catch a plane to Heathrow, arriving early to give myself plenty of time. The staff at Vietnam Airlines, however, had other ideas.

There appeared to be a problem as I'd not arrived on a connecting flight from Danang. This was where I'd first flown to 8 weeks earlier, but because I hadn't checked in at Danang, they informed me I would have to pay for another seat. I explained that I'd missed the plane but was here to take the second flight back to the UK, for which I also held a ticket.

I'd paid for a return seat on the Danang flight that I hadn't used, and I had paid for another seat on VN51 to Heathrow. The airline wasn't out of pocket so why the problem? Clearly, it wasn't a lack of available seats, as they now wanted me to pay for a second one.

The rude, unhelpful staff were adamant I had to pay again, and I spent the next hour running back and forth between their office and check-in desk in a state of increasing exasperation. The airline was blackmailing me into buying another ticket as unless I paid they wouldn't allow me on the plane and I would be stuck in Vietnam. Obviously, that wasn't an option for me, and they knew it. In the end, there was little I could do but hand over my credit card.

So despite the close call with a pickpocketing petty criminal in Cambodia, there was no escaping professional ones working for Vietnam Airlines at the airport!

Early Travels: Yugoslavia 1985

Young. Dumb. Machine gun

THE TIME WAS close to midnight and apart from the floodlit foreground, it was pitch black. Wearing camouflage military jackets we were sitting in shadows, hidden from sight outside a restaurant and tourist gift shop. Both of which were closed. A large security guard was approaching, his patrol route bringing him straight towards us... And he was carrying a machine gun!

To make the scenario even worse, neither of us spoke a word of Serbo-Croatian...

AND YET THE day had started so well. Our campsite was idyllic, nestled alongside rugged Adriatic coastline, with just a cluster of colourful tents pitched under shady trees. The sun was shining, the temperature perfect. Time had little significance.

Having got back late from a local disco, my old school friend Brad and I, enjoyed a languid breakfast before heading off mid-morning. Our plan for the day being a visit to a national park at Plitvice.

A short hop on a quiet bus took us to Rijeka where we jumped aboard a train bound for our destination. Two and a half hours later we arrived... Or so we thought until we noticed a sign. In fact, we'd only made as far as Ogulin and now needed another train.

A slow, uncomfortable hour or so passed before we got off again, glad to be leaving the unpadded wooden seats behind. But then we discovered we needed a coach to take us on to Plitvice, which wouldn't be departing for another ninety minutes!

By now it was approaching late afternoon and reality dawned it was likely the park would be closed by the time we reached it. When our coach finally arrived, we'd come up with a plan and decided to spend the night in town and visit the park the following morning. However, our plan turned out to have a flaw and a major one at that…

After some time aboard the coach, I spotted a small Plitvice sign by a huddle of buildings and assumed it to be the outskirts of town. But thirty minutes later we'd seen little else and realised perhaps there was no town! With no language skills, nobody to ask and now anxious not to leave Plitvice behind, we got the driver to pull over and stepped down onto the dark empty road. And began to walk back the way we had come. It was to be the start of a lot of walking that night…

FIVE WEEKS EARLIER we left British shores with vague dreams of a six-month working holiday starting in France. Two naïve twenty-one-year-olds with a taste for adventure and a few hundred quid in our pockets. No plans. No guidebooks. No worries. But also no command of French, or any other language and no idea about travel!

Being the mid-eighties, this was well before the advent of the Internet, which meant no smartphones, no trip advisor, no hostelbookers. In a nutshell, no easy access to information. How we even learned of the park's existence I don't know, perhaps we'd seen a nice picture somewhere and thought it looked worth a visit! But we were young, lacking life experience, and back home lived with mums who sorted most things out!

So there we were plodding our way down the lonely road, stomachs rumbling in protest as we hadn't bothered to bring anything aside from a couple of apples and a bag or two of crisps. We found a solitary roadside diner and devoured most of everything on offer before hitting the tarmac once more. There was no way of knowing how far our coach had travelled so all we could do was keep walking.

After three hours we finally got back to the park entrance. The desolate road hadn't filled us with confidence we would find much open, but we still harboured hopes of finding beds for the night. The sight of nothing but a few unlit locked buildings soon shattered that!

It was late, getting cold and now we had nowhere to sleep. We couldn't recall seeing anything on the road further ahead, so that gave us a choice, albeit not a good one. Stay put, or keep walking in the slim hope of finding somewhere else. Outside the buildings was little except a few wooden tables and chairs, but as we'd walked for so long, we elected to stay.

Facing the restaurant was an open-fronted shed, so we dragged chairs into the back and slumped down with the expectation of a long cold night. It felt great to sit down after our long trudge, and at least we could rest our legs and maybe doze for a few hours.

That was until we spotted the guard. The guard with a gun.

WE WERE IN the shadows, so he couldn't see us, or so I hoped. He was still a distance away but walking towards us. In front, floodlights illuminated everything, so we couldn't move without being seen. We had no options; we needed to stay put. I prayed he would change his course or turn around. But he kept approaching.

I whispered "pretend to be asleep", reluctantly shut my eyes and rested my head against Brad's shoulder. My pounding heart sounded so loud that I thought the guard would hear it and was desperate to flick open an eye but knew I mustn't.

Minutes passed. They felt like hours. The path would bring him right past. It didn't seem possible he wouldn't see us. Or hear my heartbeat.

When I could bear it no longer I enacted a silent wake up. Slow lifting of reluctant lids, unfocused eyes, sleepy stretching. All the while praying he wasn't there, but thinking this needed to be convincing if he was.

I couldn't see him. I nudged Brad. We scanned the scene before us; definitely no sign of the security guard.

We looked at each other and made a signal. Nodded agreement. And ran. Fast.

As the adrenaline wore off and our elation subsided, reality came seeping back. Now we had neither seats nor shelter, and it was bitterly cold. Also, had the guard seen us? Were more on their way? Our young imaginations ran riot in the lonely night.

So we kept walking, again. We crossed a bridge and scrambled down the bank seeking sanctuary below, but the stench sent us clambering straight back up to the road. Goats must have liked the shelter too, as it was littered with piles of their poo.

Most of the night was spent walking to stay warm whilst searching for somewhere to sleep. We found an isolated hotel and banged on the door. It opened, but not for long. Two foreigners in military combat jackets arriving well after midnight without luggage; little wonder the door closed in our faces!

Later, we came across a bus shelter with a bench inside and slumped down to doze. In the half-light of pre-dawn, I awoke to find a stranger seated next to me and quickly started walking again!

At dawn, we retraced our footsteps to the park, climbed its gates and ventured in. Steps led us down to a beautiful mist-shrouded river valley, where a snaking wooden walkway rose above crystal-clear water dappled with rising trout. Gurgling waterfalls cascaded around us from lush verdant forest lining the valley. Birdsong filled the air.

But despite the sublime setting, we felt too shattered to explore further and soon climbed back over the gates and left before the park even opened.

Due to an infrequency of trains, it took the rest of the day to retrace the route and we didn't get back to our tent until around ten. By then, for the first time, I was really looking forward to lying on my thin roll mat on baked, stony ground, beneath sweaty canvas inside our tiny cramped tent!

OUR SIX-MONTH TRIP turned out to be somewhat more short-lived in the end. Seven weeks after leaving home we found ourselves back on British soil once more. Our cheap backpacks had broken, we looked skinnier than when we left and were now both skint! We had failed to hitchhike far, failed to find work of any sort and failed to leave the UK for long.

On the other hand, we'd travelled to seven countries, met people from all over Europe, avoided getting shot or arrested and had an amazing adventure!

OUR SHORT TRIP really gave me an early taste for travel… But in retrospect, it seems that it taught me little about planning!

On the treacherous slopes of Kelimutu I got lost amongst the volcano's near-impenetrable jungle vegetation and, as a new author on Amazon, it will be easy for my book to share a similar fate and get lost amongst the millions of others available. Tom Tom Corner has been many years in the making and two years in the writing, so if you enjoyed my stories please take a few moments to leave a review.

Happy travels!

48108791R00200

Printed in Poland
by Amazon Fulfillment
Poland Sp. z o.o., Wrocław